INTERNATIONAL BESTSELLER

PURPOSE DRIVEN PAYCHECK

Transform your paycheck into
a tool for ~~survival~~ success

GINA REDZANIC

Along with 18 inspirational
success stories

ISBN: 978-1-960136-19-0

Table of Contents

INTRODUCTION

Purpose Driven Paycheck is an anthology of 18 unique chapters demonstrating the grit and determination of individuals who took a leap of faith to build their work, career, or business around their passion. The project lead, Gina Redzanic, has been in the entrepreneurial space for over 15 years and has a passion for inspiring others to pursue a purpose-driven career. Gina is a speaker and business coach, helping individuals and small businesses find success by leaning on their own self-confidence, strengths, and skills.

In today's society, many adults are working a job they are not happy with; many even loathe their job and are riddled with stress daily. Finding work that provides a paycheck but also serves as a passion or purpose may seem like a rare occurrence, but it is becoming the desire of more and more working adults. In this book, you will learn tangible tips from incredible authors while also diving deeper into their journey to finding their purpose. Readers will be encouraged to make their life's work feel meaningful and rewarding.

Each author's story is unique and was carefully selected to provide hope and support to the reader. The raw and real stories shared within this book are sure to provide a dose of inspiration.

Gina Redzanic

Income Strategist/Business Coach

Gina Redzanic is a certified Business and Success Coach, published author, and income strategist. Gina is happily married raising two daughters in North Carolina.

Gina initially dove into entrepreneurship in 2008, when she and her husband started their own fitness business from the trunk of their car! She went on to build her own 7-figure organization in network marketing and continued to commit herself to further education in personal and business development.

Gina has been featured in many publications like Yahoo! Finance, Brainz Magazine, and was named Top 10 Leadership Coaches in Influencive Magazine. Prior to taking the lead on the anthology, "Purpose Driven Paycheck," Gina was a contributing author in the best-selling network marketing book series, "Momentum Makers" and the best-selling series "Becoming an Unstoppable Woman." Gina specializes in helping her clients build their brand and their self-confidence in business, while building their income.

https://www.linkedin.com/in/gina-redzanic/
https://www.facebook.com/gina.pantanoredzanic
https://www.instagram.com/the.self.confidence.coach
www.ginaredzanic.com

BE A BOSS, MARRY A BOSS, BUILD A DREAM LIFE

By Gina Redzanic

"Build your dream life!" Sounds so cliché, am I right? What is a "dream life" anyway? I believe that depends on who you ask. When I met my husband, Rod, we talked a lot about our future and what this life together would look like. For us, our vision was to be fully present to experience the joys of life. We wanted to enjoy each other and also be present with the family we planned to create.

Being a dreamer and marrying a dreamer can be challenging! To be fully transparent, many times in our lives we let our desires overshadow logic. At the core of everything, we held on to our vision, which was to create a family dynamic where our work was an exciting part of what we do, but not something that would control decisions, or keep us from each other and our family. I am proud to say that, together as a couple, we achieved that vision and are living a life full of purpose.

Managing the highs and lows of business building, along with raising a family, takes grit, determination and a whole lot of belief.

Prior to finding our own path to creating a purpose-driven paycheck, work was quite different. I graduated from college with a teaching degree and taught elementary education for seven years before leaving to give corporate America a try. Rod had a Master's degree in finance and went on to work as a money manager. While dating, we were both part of the 9-5 grind and our conversations always seemed to be about how we would create a life where work was more on our terms, about our passions, and on our schedule. Even though we changed our course, we are grateful for the education and experience we gained from our previous jobs.

Going "All In" on Entrepreneurship

When passion is ignited, our gifts are discovered. Rod and I were both passionate about fitness and health and exercising was not only an interest, but a part of our everyday life. After we were married, as a hobby, we held fitness "boot camp" classes because Rod was also a certified fitness trainer, and we wanted to bring our passion to others. We did this for free while working our full-time jobs.

A pivotal point in our journey was when I was eight months pregnant with our first daughter. The economy was hurting, and many companies were laying off employees. I was one of them! I decided to enjoy the end of my pregnancy and perhaps be a stay-at-home mom. But when our daughter was four months old, Rod was laid off too! Jobs were slim and Rod desperately wanted to leave the desk job for a fitness career. Hesitant initially, I decided to go "all in" with him and build a fitness business. We turned his hobby "boot camp" classes into a business. This was 2009, and Rod was actually a pioneer of the concept of "boot camp" classes in the fitness realm. Over the next three years, we had wiped through our savings, created debt, and had to let investment properties foreclose. While doing what we loved as business owners, beneath the surface we were stressed and struggling financially. At this time, we also were expecting our second daughter. Desperate to help our financial situation, we tried to expand the fitness business into other locations, but found rather than increasing our income, it actually cost us more money and did not give us the result we desired.

I will never forget the day I opened our savings account to transfer the $2,000 needed to pay bills, which I did every month, and noticed this was the final $2,000. Our credit cards were maxed and now our savings account was almost empty. We quickly realized that entrepreneurship had its challenges and we recognized the importance of creating multiple streams of income and having smart investments in place.

Along Came Network Marketing

The year was 2013, and I was a bit ignorant about network marketing. I had been approached by networkers before and the tactics did not connect with me. However, I discovered a nutrition line with results I could not deny, and I saw the benefit of offering a nutrition recommendation with our fitness business. Immediately I was earning the $2,000 a month we needed to make ends meet! After two and a half years earning an additional $2,000 to $3,000 monthly, Rod and I decided to go to a company event. This event gave us an up close and personal view of the ownership, the integrity, the compensation plan, and mainly the possibility of a serious income stream. We got to work on our own beliefs, our skills, and our business plan. Rod took over most of the fitness business duties which allowed me time to start over and build a business the right way! Two years later, we were on stage as six-figure income earners. The income allowed us to repair our credit and start saving again. After eight years of owning our Florida-based fitness business, we sold it to relocate to North Carolina. Rod continued to work as an independent trainer and manage our investments, but we were full-time with our network marketing business. We were able to build a home in North Carolina, which was the first home we were able to buy as a married couple! Most importantly, we experienced the freedom this lifestyle offered, and we were able to raise our daughters while being totally present in their lives.

Recognizing our Gifts

I began to grow increasingly passionate about leadership development and helping others become more self-confident. 2020 was a transitional year globally, and it was a time for deep reflection and an opportunity to pivot. I decided to focus more on leadership skills and create more leverage for myself to help people in business and entrepreneurship. I completed the Maxwell Leadership Certification course, became a contributing author and writer on several projects, and created a forum that would serve aspiring entrepreneurs and business owners. Rod focused more on his financial background and roots and grew our investment portfolio. Together, we never faltered from our vision of being a family who is present and experiencing life together. It was a season of life where we grew closer to recognizing our own talents and how to best serve others using those gifts.

Conclusion: Paying it Forward

Today, Rod and I use our entire experience to further feed our purpose. Our journey has not only shaped us but has equipped us with knowledge and actual experience to better serve others who have a goal to live life with a dose of freedom and financial security. There are hills and valleys, and while the journey was far from perfect, it has been absolutely rewarding. Creating our purpose-driven paycheck has meant we never missed a field trip, school play, and never had to ask someone for time off. Creating a financial portfolio together to set up our future has meant knowing when to take some risks and recognizing the importance of budgeting. During times when we became stuck or struggled on our next steps, we always returned to our initial vision for our life and trusted in the next opportunities and ventures to get us there.

Expert Tips: Time Management Strategies

Working together as a couple and diversifying in many areas was only possible because of our attention to time management strategies. The following strategies have allowed us to increase productivity, reduce stress, have control of workflow, and consistently meet deadlines.

- Plan your day

   Planning your day in a calendar is one of the best ways to stay on task. I like to use highlighters and highlight tasks based on topic. For example, work tasks are green, personal appointments are yellow, family/kids are pink. I also keep a master "To Do" list on my desk. When I have time on my calendar to work, I simply start ticking away at the list based on order of priority.

- Divide larger projects into smaller tasks

One of the most common reasons people don't manage their time well on large projects is that they feel overwhelmed. When you feel overwhelmed, you may want to procrastinate and work on other things instead. To overcome this feeling, break large projects into smaller, more manageable tasks.

- Limit distractions

Everyone gets distracted. Whether it's email, social media, kids, or random thoughts, countless things can interrupt your progress. When you schedule time to work, guard that time, set a timer, and commit to focusing on the tasks without getting distracted.

- Reduce multitasking tasks

Multitasking can actually lead to being more overwhelmed and cause you to be less productive. I personally had to learn the skill of NOT multitasking. Once I created better habits of finishing one task before moving on, it helped relieve stress and create more productivity.

- Block time off on your calendar

Keeping all of your events, meetings, deadlines, and tasks on your calendar can save you time. Having a single place to check these things saves time. Online calendar apps such as Google Calendar and Calendly are an even more efficient way to schedule time. The ability to check your calendar across different devices and set reminders adds to this time management strategy's effectiveness.

- Summarize and review your day

  At the end of the day, it's time to reflect on what you accomplished and set yourself up for success the following day. This is the perfect time to review your to-do list from that day to see all of the items you checked off and what is still left to be tackled tomorrow. The end-of-day review is also a chance for honest self-reflection about how well you managed your time that day. Through self-reflection, you can identify what's working and where you can continue to improve.

- Rest and Recharge

  Make sure you add downtime for self-care in your day. If you are working on devices like a phone or computer throughout the day, taking breaks to move around will serve you greatly. When you begin to feel drained or stressed from work, be sure to give yourself some grace. This is a good time to go for a walk, sit on a porch, or meditate for a few minutes.

Nichole Rea

CEO of Nichole Marie Collective

In 2009, Nichole Rea accepted her first position as a graduate Registered Nurse. During the first 4 years, Nichole grew in her profession and flourished. However by 2012, it was clear that healthcare was changing. Inadequate staffing was a daily issue, and nurses were expected to care for more patients, with less ancillary staff to support the rise in patient numbers.

This pressure, along with the desire to care for more critical patients, encouraged Nichole to accept a position in an intensive care unit at another hospital. Unfortunately, staffing issues among healthcare facilities continued to worsen. The ability to safely care for her patients became harder and harder for Nichole, creating an unhealthy work environment.

Nichole eventually resigned from the hospital and began her journey as an entrepreneur in 2016. She is an internationally published photographer, owns a 6-figure studio, and encourages people to grow in authenticity and confidence.

www.facebook.com/Mrs.NicholeRea
www.instagram.com/hellonicholerea
www.nicholemariecollective.com

MY 3-STEP RECIPE FOR PERSONAL SUCCESS

By Nichole Rea

Had someone told me 10 years ago that I'd be sitting down today at the dining room table in my dream home to write a chapter for a book about how I left my professional career as a registered nurse to take photos of women in lingerie, I probably would have had severe anxiety followed by a panic attack! Back then, quitting my job at the hospital seemed ludicrous, considering how much effort I had put into getting through nursing school. Back then, paying off the sixty thousand dollars of debt my husband and I had racked up seemed impossible. Back then, I felt trapped.

But here I sit writing that very chapter, so you know that shit happened, and the only person I have to thank for my continued success is me.

As you begin to read this, some of you may argue that my husband, Mark, also played a significant role in creating the life we currently live, and he did! But for the purpose of this chapter, when I say I am the only one to thank for my success, I'm talking about personal, internal success that continues to flourish throughout my existence on this planet.

Let me start by saying that I am constantly evaluating my dream life. The motivation I need to keep myself going when life ebbs and flows into a bad chapter comes from within me. And the confidence required to take the leap of faith towards a big decision when no one else thinks it will work comes from within me; and that's the message I'm here to share with you now.

The future is quite literally limitless, but until I discovered my own recipe for success, I stayed in the scary, uncomfortable, stressful, monotonous cycle I was in. Thankfully for you, you're reading this book, which tells me you're curious to learn how we authors got out of the trap, and built a life around doing what we love so that you can too! So, let's dive in.

Years ago, when I started paying attention to how I felt for the twelve hours I was working my shift in ICU when there wasn't enough staff, or the twelve hours I worked on holidays because I didn't make my own work schedule, I realized that I was moving through life the way someone else was allowing me to. I was given a schedule I had to follow whether I liked it or not, or I risked losing my job. I showed up at work and was assigned a number of patients based on what the hospital thought was appropriate, but was given no say on what I felt I could personally, safely handle. I was having bouts of anxiety driving to work, asking myself, "Will today be the day one of my patient's dies because I have no one to help me save them?"

This process of stopping to identify how I felt and why I felt that way is step one in my recipe for personal success: Make time for self exploration. The more frequently I check in with myself, the more frequently I become aware of my reality and how it's affecting me. I ask myself on a regular basis how I feel, I define my passions, and I define my poisons. The passions get illuminated, the poisons get eliminated.

Once I identified how I felt about my position in the hospital, my next step was to determine what I could do about it. I felt bullied, stressed, and was constantly in fear of losing my license, but unfortunately the actions that needed to be taken in order to fix the continual issues were out of my control, so I decided to find another source of income. This way, I could eventually quit my job as a nurse altogether.

Step two in my recipe for personal success is: Take responsibility. When I knew in the pit of my stomach that I had to leave nursing, it was overwhelming to say the least. I was scared, and I thought I would let people down, especially Mark. But I also knew myself, and the situation I was in wasn't healthy for me anymore. I had defined my poison.

It was around this time that I started thinking about what I liked to do in my free time; what made me feel curious and excited? I had always wanted to learn photography, and even took a class in high school, but I never made time to put anything I learned into practice. So I started researching photography 101, and my passion was reignited. My brain was a sponge, and I couldn't think about anything else during my free time. I watched hours of YouTube videos, and spent my days off practicing by taking photos of my kids playing in the yard, or around the house, so I could learn how to use my camera. I taught myself how to edit, how to use Photoshop and Lightroom, and how to market my work on social media. Every time I saw some artistic growth in my work, I would become more and more excited about what I was doing. I was filling up my own cup doing something that didn't feel like work at all, which was amazing and foreign at the same time.

Eventually I started taking photos of other people, and the shift from nurse to photographer slowly began to happen. I took classes geared towards teaching photographers how to build a profitable business and built my own website. I created a pricing structure that was appropriate for my services and used the profit I made to upgrade to professional gear, buy a better computer, and invested in tons of other things I would need to start my own business.

At this time I was still working as a nurse, but every other weekend I was a photographer doing shoots out of our own home. We had two children under the age of 3, and I was pregnant with our third, but the momentum behind me was so strong that I couldn't slow it down.

Word got out about what I was charging for my services, and some people began to respond negatively. A co-worker in the hospital asked me what I would charge to photograph his son's wedding. When I gave him my price, he rolled his eyes, shook his head, and walked away.

Receiving negative reactions like that sent me very confusing messages. On one hand, I was personally challenging myself to continually get better, and seeing leaps in my own progress!! I was so proud of myself and what I had accomplished, elated even! But on the other hand, when I shared my work and felt a sense of pride, only to be told that I wasn't "worth it," even in non-verbal ways like eye-rolling, the pride diminished and embarrassment took its place.

I started second guessing myself and my own gut feeling about the luxury experience I was creating, and the quality of my hard work, even though I knew better. My confidence dwindled, and it was hard at times to keep going. But this is where I learned my most valuable and difficult lesson: Maintain confidence in yourself, and all that you do, even when no one else does.

During the end of my time working in the hospital, people told me not to leave nursing. But when the comments were spoken and the judgements were made, at the end of the day I knew what my own personal success looked like. With a beautiful photography studio in mind, I continued working towards my goals. I had done my research, put in the work, taken my time, carefully planned out my expenses, and I knew what "success" meant for me! So regardless of what anyone said, that feeling deep in my stomach kept pushing me forward, saying "Nah girl, you got this! You know what you're doing. Keep fucking going!"

My photography company was born in January of 2015, Mark encouraged me to quit my nursing job in August of 2016, and in June of 2021, after my studio's third six-figure year, we spent our first night in our brand new home. At the time of publishing, I will have been in business for 8 years, and serviced over 1000 clients. I am now on the brink of another milestone in my life, and am continuing to ask myself,

"How do I feel right now?" But this time is a bit different, because I now have the recipe for my own personal success, and I excitedly await the discovery of my next "purpose."

Expert Tips:

Once you make the decision to start moving towards the dreams that will inevitably bring about your unique personalized version of success, it can start to get overwhelming or even scary. You might feel alone or lost in regards to what you should be focusing on, so use the following tips when you need to get yourself back on track.

- The first thing to do when working towards a new goal is to find a source of support. This doesn't have to be super structured with scheduled meetings or appointments. Something as simple as joining a Facebook group with people who are working towards the same goals will be super helpful when you find yourself needing to vent or looking for advice.

- My next tip is this: When you get to a point in your journey where you feel overwhelmed because you're unsure about what you should be learning or doing, it's really important to define only the next step. What is the very next thing that you need to do? When I was working towards leaving nursing, it was overwhelming thinking about how I would be able to afford a studio to work out of, find locations to shoot at, and store my files so they were protected. But the first thing I needed to do was learn how to use my camera! All of the other details would come later. The only thing I needed to start doing was practicing.

- My final and last tip for you (and this is the one that will really help you keep your head up when things get hard), is to remember that you are only in competition with yourself! You simply can not compare your work, your progress, or your accomplishments with anyone else, because they are not you. Keep your head down, and in your own lane. Following other people as sources of inspiration is fine, but you will most likely feel down on yourself about how slow you're moving, or how amateur your work is. Remember when that happens that everyone starts at the bottom, and as long as you stay focused, eventually you too will rise to the top. Your personal success is totally achievable, all you have to do is define it, believe it, and work towards it, one step at a time.

Christina Motta

Wellness & Wealth Advocate

Christina Motta, self described as an 'accidental entrepreneur,' has enjoyed eight years of incredible growth and expansion on this unexpected journey. Christina lives in Dutchess County, NY with her husband and two teenage daughters. She earned a Master's degree in Health Education, and did her undergraduate work in Physical Education and Outdoor Environmental Education. Concluding her 23rd school year as a Physical Education & Health Teacher, Christina loves sharing her passions with students and clients.

Christina's mission is to help those feeling like they have a bigger purpose, and want to grow and serve in powerful ways. She desires to assist families that value wellness, who may be capped in income or want to create financial breathing room and ease financial stress by using a side business as a vehicle. Christina is looking to work with those who are passionate about people, about wellness, and who value collaboration over competition.

https://www.linkedin.com/in/christina-chrissy-motta-9957a9268/
https://www.facebook.com/christina.motta.58
https://www.instagram.com/chrissymotta/
www.christina-motta.com

RISE & SHINE

By Christina Motta

"Your talent is God's gift to you.
What you do with it is your gift back to God."
—Leo Buscaglia

In my 45 years on this planet, I have come to a conclusion: What brings you joy can never be wrong. If you want to find your purpose and live a passion-driven life, you have to give your attention and take some time to reflect on the things or experiences that give you high vibration feelings and not worry about what loved ones or others think you are 'supposed' to do. Happiness flows easier that way—so does money. Remember that those people with opinions are not paying your bills, fulfilling your dreams, or helping you contribute to the charities that have your heart.

From my earliest memories I can remember feeling joy in my body anytime I helped someone in some way. Not necessarily when I was asked to or told to; when it came from within, my heart was happiest. Connecting with others gave me a wave of exhilaration. Choosing to live a life of service and becoming a teacher came as no surprise to me, though becoming an entrepreneur, something I never associated with service or connection earlier in my life, was not something I expected or foresaw, which is why it is so awesome, scary, and exciting! Choosing to study Physical & Outdoor Education and pursue a Master's degree in Health Education felt very natural and was an easy path to pursue because it combined my passions for health & wellness, nature, and teaching. Growing up I was blessed to have some of the most incredible and unforgettable teachers and coaches, and they had a profound impact on my life. The idea of paying it forward was attractive and once I began my studies, I was confident I had made the right decision.

Witnessing as students grasp a concept, learn a new skill, make connections, encourage each other, strategize, work and laugh together…these are the moments that are the absolute best and why after 23 years of teaching I still love what I do. However, for years I experienced this *pull* that there was something more. In pursuit of challenge and growth, I joined various committees at the District Office level, and I grew, but it didn't feel aligned with my values; I found myself again asking and praying for my purpose to be revealed….and just like that, when I least expected it, a question was asked of me by a friend. In that moment, a seed was planted and I was oblivious to the impact it would have on me and others. It wasn't a mind blowing question, it was really a small pebble thrown in the water that would later have a tremendous ripple effect on my life. My friend asked me to join her on her wellness journey using some really great science based products. Initially, I said "no, thank you."

Six months later I found myself an exhausted working mom of two young girls, giving all the energy I could muster to my students and having nothing left for my family at the end of the day. My "go-to" lifelong strategies were not working, and my daily workouts weren't reaping the physical or mental stress-relieving results I had known my whole life. It also happened to be the holiday season, which compounded the financial stress of living paycheck to paycheck. I had hit a wall and prayed for things to turn around.

INSERT—God's perfect timing.

That seed planted six months prior started to bloom! An opportunity to be in the company of that same friend, on a day I was feeling all the feels, changed everything. I finally said "yes" and joined her on a health journey. Beautiful surprises and blessings were on the horizon for my family and I, and I was completely unaware.

Being introduced to a system and set of products eight years ago became a solution to my exhaustion (and helped me build some real lean muscle, which was exciting), but the profound experience that would change the course of my life was that my friend had *interrupted my pattern of thinking* about how to earn money when she casually mentioned the opportunity to assist others in feeling as good as I was.

My backstory regarding money is simple: I grew up in a blue collar environment and was raised by people who had an incredible work ethic and who worked overtime hours whenever they could. I saw the stress finances could cause, so I grew up wanting to contribute, to help out and lighten the load by being able to take care of myself. I worked numerous jobs from a young age in between sports seasons and during the summer, and in college found myself working several jobs at once. Hustle and grind. I was good at it. I felt accomplished, and proud that I didn't have to ask my parents for money very often. That 'hustle and grind' mentality served me well; I was hired as a full time Physical Education teacher right out of school, was offered two sport coaching positions, and hit the ground running by starting my Master's degree at the same time. The people I worked for throughout my life always appreciated that mentality; I made life easy for them, as I was never an employee anyone had to worry about. I always went above and beyond.

When entrepreneurship entered my life my mentality began to shift. The work ethic didn't go away, but everything started to feel different—because 'personal development' was a huge part of my training as an entrepreneur. I felt a shift, so I started to invest in myself even more. I went to work on understanding my beliefs around money, time, and seeing myself as a businesswoman. I was also shown how to work on being present, and I realized I didn't have to 'hustle and grind' to earn money; what mattered was having a clear vision, being intentional with my time, creating boundaries, protecting my energy, and surrounding myself with optimistic, reflective, reliable, and growth-oriented people.

The truth is, I had no idea what the Network Marketing business model was or that this industry even existed. The opportunity fell into my lap simply by falling in love with the products I was putting into my body. This business model is not for everyone, but it was what allowed me to turn my passion and purpose into a business; it required very little start-up capital and the systems and marketing were done for me. Unlike a 'brick and mortar' business where you start from scratch and handle every detail, in the Network Marketing industry all of the 'behind the scenes' work is done for you. When you are someone who is juggling a career, family life and activities, and keeping up a household, this model can be EXTREMELY attractive.

How impressive that in this particular business model, and in my particular company, the marketing, business systems, the third-party testing and integrity of products, the compensation plan, paying out of your team, etc. is all taken care of for you? Music to my ears! You mean I can still enjoy my teaching career, run a business and earn a substantial supplemental income and not worry about any of the other stuff?! Game on! Remember, I didn't go to college for business and that 'other stuff' is certainly not my passion. This business model turned out to be a fantastic fit for me to create an additional stream of income outside of my teaching career.

With Network Marketing you can earn while you learn, which is fantastic. If you plan to become any type of entrepreneur, while your passion and work ethic are great assets, they will only take you so far. *Investing in yourself* is the secret sauce, particularly investing in your mindset and your belief in yourself. BELIEF IS EVERYTHING. Our thoughts create our reality and there is no way around that.

One of the biggest factors and skills that determines your success in the Network Marketing industry is the art of connection. Talking to, caring about, and serving people is the meat and potatoes of this industry. For many, like myself, that feels and sounds very natural, but it was a huge surprise witnessing how challenging it was. I realized quickly that there is so much junk in our heads about what other people will think, which holds us back and gets in the way of our success. When you go to work on letting go of others' opinions, that's when the magic begins. Trust me, invest in yourself. It is worth every penny and not only influences your business but your relationships with those you love most.

Becoming an entrepreneur requires many leaps of faith, letting go of old stories, giving up control and allowing people, places, and things to enter your experience whether you envisioned them or not.

Never in a million years would I have expected to be writing a chapter in an entrepreneurial book, but I trusted that when the opportunity presented itself, it was for a reason. I was welcomed to join this project and it surprised me to see how excited I felt about it. When you truly 'ALLOW' and let go, you will be shown the path. I have to admit, so much of this journey in entrepreneurship has not been what I pictured it would be—it has been SO much better!

It's time to *Rise & Shine* my friend. Show up in the process and 'GO FOR IT!'

If you are reading this book, this is YOUR moment!

Expert Tips:

Invest in Yourself and Witness the Magic

> *"Your greatness is limited only by the investments*
> *you make in yourself."*
> —Grant Cardone

Investing in yourself means putting the time, money, and energy into making your current life better.

- Take Care of Your Body

  If you are going to be taking on entrepreneurship and want to do it well, you have to prioritize your health. 'Your vibe will attract your tribe.' Focus on nutrition, water intake, moving your body & sleep. *(I can help you with this.)*

- Do the Mind and Soul Work

  The bookends of your day can be really powerful. Kickstart and end your day in an aligned state. It does not require a lot of time, it requires *conscious* and *intentional* time. Set your alarm 15-30 minutes early and intentionally use that time for your own personal development. Do the same before bed. Some of my favorite go-to activities: read five pages of a book, meditate, write in my gratitude journal, and Daily Devotionals.

- Listen to Podcasts for Personal Development & Entrepreneurship

  There are so many incredible podcasts out there. Some of my favorites include: Gabby Bernstein, Mel Robbins, The Ed Mylett Show, and ITFactor with Emily Ford. I listen to them on my commute, on a morning or lunchtime run/walk, waiting for my children to get out from practice, etc. Take advantage of the time you have by yourself to grow yourself.

- Hire a Coach!

  This is where I have witnessed the most growth because of the financial investment and accountability. Talk to people that have hired a coach for a recommendation based on what you are looking for. Be ready for some life changing experiences and maturation! When you hire someone and make that financial exchange of money, you are sending a strong message to God/the universe.

- Go to/Create Events!

  Entrepreneurship 101: *People buy from those they know, like, and trust.* Period.

  Attend networking events, go to company events, search 'meet-up' groups, put yourself out there and meet people! CONNECT and then connect on a deeper level. If you can't find events to attend, create your own! Go to your local Facebook community groups, etc. Create a poll to see who would be interested. People want to be part of a community. If you build it, they will come. Be okay with and grateful for a small number of people to start. Over time the numbers will grow. The people you connect with may or may not become future customers or teammates, but they will refer you and referrals build your business.

Becky Skeba- Mancini

Re/Max Services The Skeba Team
Realtor

Becky Skeba-Mancini, a passionate entrepreneur since 2004, has dedicated her life to the world of Real Estate. Becky's journey as a young mom-turned-entrepreneur fuels her passion for success.

As a single mom of three children, Becky has mastered the art of balancing parenthood with her successful Real Estate career.

Becky is a valued member of The Skeba Team, a top producing Residential and Commercial Team. The Skeba team has been the 3rd ranked Commercial team in the entire U.S for Re/Max and has been nominated as Commercial Broker of the year in their local MLS.

Becky and her team redefine industry standards, leveraging their vast knowledge and innovative strategies to deliver unparalleled service.

Alongside her real estate expertise, Becky is also the host of the popular podcast, Selling Success.

In her free time, she cherishes moments spent with her children, explores new places, and actively engages with her community.

www.linkedin.com/in/rebecca-skeba-mancini-36495725
https://www.facebook.com/profile.php?id=100006068805149
https://www.instagram.com/becky.skebamancini/
www.skebamancini.com

TRIUMPH OVER ADVERSITY: UNLEASHING SELLING SUCCESS AGAINST ALL ODDS

By Becky Skeba- Mancini

In life, we often encounter unexpected challenges that test our resilience and determination. This chapter is a deeply personal account of my journey to selling success, overcoming the hurdles of becoming a parent at 20, and living through a life-altering divorce. Through these experiences, I have grown, learned, and transformed, ultimately emerging as a resilient individual capable of achieving remarkable success. In sharing my story, I hope to inspire and guide you on your own path towards sales excellence, even in the face of what seem to be obstacles. Join me as I share my story and empower you to overcome negative expectations and realize your true potential.

I have turned many of life's challenges into opportunities by learning to embrace life's curveballs. Life has a funny way of testing us. I embraced motherhood at the age of 19. Becoming a parent at such a young age was undoubtedly a shock. However, I quickly realized that this new responsibility was an opportunity for growth. Despite the challenges, I embraced the journey of motherhood with determination and resilience. The love and dedication I poured into raising my child fueled my drive to create a better future for us both. Throughout my life, I have encountered individuals who tried to define my worth and limit my potential. I defied the expectations placed upon me by those who doubted my abilities. From being told I would amount to nothing and become a statistic, I have risen above adversity, proving that one's success is not determined by others' limited perceptions. Through sheer determination, resilience, and a refusal to accept mediocrity, I have surpassed expectations and achieved remarkable success in the world of real estate.

At 39, I lived through a divorce and left behind a successful career in a multimillion-dollar company to start over from scratch. I wasn't sure that I was making the right decision; I was leaving a situation in which I was very comfortable. Through resilience, determination, and a willingness to embrace change, I not only rebuilt my life but also achieved remarkable success. I am now a valued member of The Skeba Team, a top producing Residential and Commercial Real Estate team. We have been ranked as the top third commercial team in the entire US for Re/Max.

When I left the company I had with my ex-husband, I felt I was going to lose everything. I couldn't believe that I had made the decision to give him the company. But then something clicked—I had had two other successful businesses; it wasn't the business itself that was a success—it was me. I was the success. I had already led two different businesses; I can do it again and I WILL.

When I first started out in real estate, there were many months where my paychecks seemed uncertain. I took the initiative to approach agents in my office, offering my assistance with showings, open houses, and inspections. I was willing to do whatever I could to make extra cash when I was just starting out. Some agents would pay me $150 to sit at an inspection. I sat at open houses hoping to secure clients who might one day purchase a property and want to hire me. I experienced months without closings, and I had so much self doubt.

I steadily built up my clientele by diligently following up with clients, maintaining a strong database, and exploring off-market commercial and residential properties. I sent monthly flyers; I did pop-bys; I spent hours on the phone calling old friends and clients. I was mentored by my broker, and we would meet every week to discuss what was and was not working.

I'm like a freight train; once I get going, I never quit. With an unstoppable drive, I push forward relentlessly, leaving no room for hesitation or complacency. Like the unyielding force of a freight train,

I refuse to be deterred by obstacles that stand in my way. I am fueled by an unwavering determination to achieve my goals, never settling for mediocrity. No matter the challenges I face, I keep pushing forward, propelling myself towards success with an unstoppable momentum. With each stride, I grow stronger and more resilient, never allowing setbacks to derail my progress. I am a force to be reckoned with, driven by an unwavering belief in my abilities and a relentless pursuit of excellence.

Another thing that helped my business was being intentional about networking. I had tried networking before and it had never worked for me; I would go out and meet people, give them my business card (and get theirs), and then I would put their cards away and never look at them again. I tried really hard to obtain as many business cards and meet as many people as I could. But this time around, I realized that I had been networking wrong the whole time. I tried a different approach—this time, when I was networking I thought not just about getting business but also about making new friends. I started to make real connections and create friendships. Instead of trying to meet everyone in the room, I would take time to look around at who I thought would like me, and who I might like. From there we could start building a relationship based on trust and likability. This worked, and the referrals came in.

Little by little I started to make relationships based on people trusting, knowing, and liking me. Now I have a database of clients—but what comes next? I use a CRM system to keep track of new clients, prospective clients, and old clients. I send out an email once a month about things of value. I call my clients and check in with them. I really get to know each one of my clients on a personal level.

I feel like I have a super power—being able to truly understand what clients want in a home or commercial property is a special ability. With an intuitive sense, I effortlessly search until I find the perfect match. I can tell just by meeting someone exactly what they are looking for—and I can usually find it. I have a keen understanding of different clients' preferences; whether a client wants an assertive agent or one who provides guidance and support, I can adapt to their needs and ensure a personalized experience.

By treating each transaction as if it were my own, I am able to make decisions with meticulous care and consider clients' best interests. I am not the kind of agent who just completes a transaction and moves on to the next client. I keep my clients for life, and they usually become friends. I know that purchasing any property, whether it be commercial or residential, can be extremely stressful, so I always try to put myself in their shoes. I treat each transaction as if it were my own purchase so that I am patient and understanding.

I started a podcast called "Selling Success," which has become a powerful catalyst for my real estate career, propelling me to new heights of success. The impact it has had on my professional growth is undeniable. Through "Selling Success" I have had the privilege of connecting with industry experts, thought leaders, and fellow real estate professionals, who have shared valuable insights and strategies that resonate with a wide audience. The positive feedback and engagement from listeners have been overwhelming, reaffirming the value of the knowledge and experiences I bring to the table. The success of my podcast has not only expanded my reach but also enhanced my credibility as a trusted authority in the real estate industry. It has opened doors to new opportunities, attracting high-profile guests and providing a platform for them to share their stories and expertise. The exponential growth of my podcast audience has translated into increased visibility, recognition, and ultimately, a significant boost in my real estate business. "Selling Success" has truly become a driving force in my career, elevating my brand and allowing me to make an even greater impact in the lives of my clients and fellow professionals.

I have triumphed over adversity in my journey to unleashing selling success against all odds. My journey is a testament to the power of perseverance, determination, and an unwavering belief in oneself. From embracing the challenges of early parenthood and a life-altering divorce to starting over from scratch and building a thriving real estate career, I have proven that setbacks can be transformed into opportunities for growth and achievement. Through resilience, diligence, and a commitment to exceeding expectations, I have overcome doubts and defied limitations. Networking and building genuine relationships have been instrumental in expanding my reach and fostering a supportive community. Additionally, my intuitive understanding of clients' needs and unwavering dedication to their best interests have established me as a trusted advisor in the industry. The success of my podcast, "Selling Success," has further amplified my impact, connecting me with industry experts and providing a platform to share valuable insights and experiences. Through it all, I remain committed to inspiring and empowering others to embrace challenges, unlock their potential, and achieve remarkable success. My journey is a testament to the resilience of the human spirit and the limitless possibilities that lie within each of us. With unwavering determination, I continue to push forward, driven by the belief that success is within reach for those who dare to dream and persevere.

Expert Tips:

- Embrace Flexibility

  Flexibility is a key component of succeeding in real estate. Balancing appointments, showings, and client meetings with your childrens' needs may seem challenging, but it's achievable with careful time management. Embrace technology that allows you to stay connected while on the go, and consider creating a flexible schedule that accommodates both work and family commitments. This way, you can be present for your childrens' important moments while excelling in your career.

- Build a Support Network

   A strong support network is essential for anyone pursuing a successful real estate career. Allow friends and family members to help you, and reach out to them if you feel like you need help. I could not do what I do everyday without the support of my family and friends. Having a reliable support system and team can make all the difference in effectively managing your personal and professional life.

- Set Realistic Goals

   Goal setting is crucial for any successful career, and real estate is no exception. It's important to set realistic and achievable goals to maintain a healthy work-life balance. Consider both short-term and long-term objectives, and break them down into manageable steps. Celebrate your achievements, no matter how small they may seem, and use setbacks as opportunities to learn and grow.

- Leverage Technology

   Technology can be your best friend in the real estate industry. Utilize tools and apps that help streamline your daily tasks, such as client management software and digital document signing services. These tools can save you time and effort, allowing you to focus more on your clients and family.

- Focus on Time Management

   Time management is critical when you have a busy real estate career and a family to care for. Create a schedule that includes dedicated time for work, family, and self-care. Prioritize your tasks, delegate when possible, and learn to say no to non-essential commitments. Effective time management will help reduce stress and ensure you can give your all to both your real estate clients and your family.

- Emphasize Open Communication

  Open communication is vital in both the real estate industry and your family life. Clearly communicate your availability to clients, colleagues, and family members to avoid any misunderstandings. If you need to reschedule appointments due to family emergencies or commitments, be honest and transparent with your clients. Most people will appreciate your honesty and flexibility.

Lacey Broocke

Lacey Broocke is a serial entrepreneur, wife, and mother currently residing in Florida. She wanted to pursue her passion in the beauty industry and decided to drop out of college. Less than four years into her beauty career, at the age of 25, Lacey fulfilled her dreams of becoming a salon and spa owner. Her talents, skills, and ambition led her to pursue yet another dream of public speaking and platform artistry, where she would join Redken, the leading beauty education team in the world. Through this position, Lacey educated thousands of stylists across the nation through her expertise!

Not content to rest on her own laurels, Lacey discovered social selling and how beneficial it was to promote products and services she uses and loves. Whether it's through the beauty industry, e-commerce or wealth building, Lacey is committed to helping others live their best life and make a living while making an impact.

https://www.linkedin.com/in/lacey-broocke-a3223824/
www.facebook.com/l.broocke
www.instagram.com/laceybroocke

WORK SMARTER, NOT HARDER

By Lacey Broocke

From the time I was a little girl, I knew two things: God is in control, and that if I wanted something I was gonna have to work for it! Being raised by a disabled mother on a cattle ranch left me no other option and I didn't know any different. I don't ever remember a time that I didn't work; I worked in the home, cleaning, cooking, taking care of the family and momma. I worked on the farm in the garden, tending the lawn and land, and yes, herding cattle (my least favorite!). By the time I was about 10 years old, I began to babysit and help family members clean and do odd jobs to make some extra money. My siblings and I desperately wanted a trampoline, so we saved our babysitting money one summer to purchase one! That was when I learned that if I wanted something I could trade my time and effort and buy whatever I wanted.

I was hired to bus tables when I was 14 and was promoted to server once I was old enough. For the first time I had NEW (not hand me down or charity) name-brand clothes! I felt so confident wearing them and paying for them myself. I went on to work 2-3 jobs at a time throughout high school to maximize my earnings. It was about this time that I was told by a guidance counselor that I shouldn't go to cosmetology school after finishing high school because I would never make enough money. The only thing I really ever wanted to do was hair and makeup, but I knew that the broke life was not for me, so I did the only thing I knew to do…I went to Community College, and then got married at 19. About a year and a half in, I read somewhere that if you love what you do then the money will come. A lightbulb went off, and I dropped college, and enrolled in the only cosmetology school I could afford.

At first I thought my guidance counselor was right! It took me a couple years to build a good clientele, and to be able to quit my waitressing job. But by 25 I was finally ready to fulfill my dream of owning a high-end salon and spa with all the bells and whistles! It really was one of the best experiences I have had, and I learned so much! I learned budgeting, planning, leading, personalities, branding, merchandising, and I learned about myself. One of my biggest lessons was loyalty (on so many levels). Brand loyalty is very important; if I used one brand I could maximize their loyalty rewards for education, products, and savings. I made the wise decision to partner with Redken, as they have everything a salon owner could possibly need (most of which I had no clue I needed). They offered education for salon owners, stylists, and every aspect of my business. I dove into as much education as I could! Then the unthinkable happened—my business partner and I had to part ways, and quite frankly I was tired of working 7am-11pm most days. I had no life, I was dealing with infertility, and my mom was dying. I was done.

After my mom passed I was left with a "normal" full time job, a husband I no longer wanted to be with, and no children. I decided to LIVE! I wanted to live my life so big! I wanted to experience everything! I wanted to be a platform artist ever since I attended my first hair show, and I was told that I couldn't do it, so I decided to audition (I've always been a rebel). I made it! Redken was my only choice, as they have the best education team in the world for our industry. I became a colourist and a wealth builder, facilitating thousands of stylists across America, sharing with them how to "Learn Better, Earn Better, and Live Best!" I shared skills and techniques to maximize earnings behind the chair, so they could live their best life. I am incredibly grateful for each and every mentor, as well as stylist, I came into contact with along the way.

And then February 2020 happened, and the world stopped… no salon clients, no classes, no shows, no money. For the first time in my life, I experienced FREEDOM. I focused on myself, my family, and GOD. I felt a shift in me, and wasn't exactly sure what it would be, but trusted that God would lead me in the right direction. I dove into my health and wellness, and my husband's—after nearly losing him in June of 2020—and people started to notice the physical changes in me. I began casually sharing my new "weight loss secrets" with those who inquired and enjoyed getting some money back on my products. But when my health & wellness company launched the world's most potent collagen, which happened to be (and still is) the hottest beauty trend, I was blown away by the results I saw on others, and decided there was no way I was going without this collagen! The company had 14 days of content that I could copy and paste to my social media to help me pay for the collagen and help others. It was a win-win!! I had so much fun and I made $800. The next week a medical bill came in the amount of $756, and I was so grateful for the money! I saw the power in social selling, as I was home with my four year old every day. I earned some trips that year, was blessed to be mentored by someone who was where I wanted to be, and met lots of new friends who really opened my eyes to time and financial freedom. There are people out there just like you and me getting paid to LIVE!! You know why? They are loyal to a brand and they believe they can do it!

Then I found my favorite workout clothing. I didn't want to wear anything else! Why not sell it?! It's fun and I can do it from anywhere! Next thing I know, my team mate (and now one of my very best friends) introduced me to a new way to help the salons I was so grateful to be going back into after being shut down for an entire year from travel and events. I began educating salon and business owners about the Employment Retention Credit, a government grant that qualifies businesses that survived COVID and retained employees up to $26k per full time employee. So wait, I can help my friends get money they didn't know was available to them AND get paid for it?! I was manifesting working less and making more money, financial abundance and favor, and every other result I wanted. And it worked!

Instead of Netflix, I studied financial education, passive income streams, investing, and personal development, and I hired a life coach who has helped me to overcome so many of my self-limiting beliefs. I cannot stress enough how important mind work is. It is VITAL for success. And I started spending more time with God, the CEO of my life. Knowing your purpose and aligning with the Holy Spirit will produce success, even if you don't recognize it at first.

I invested in E-Commerce, as well as some automated businesses that produce passive income, allowing me to be where I need and want to be when I want to be there. I found other online tools I need for my businesses and that people I'm coaching and leading need to take their business to the next level, and of course I need to be able to recommend the best. Guess what—they also have affiliate pay! When your business is everything you do, everything you do becomes a write-off.

As a mother, I want to be there for everything; but bringing home the bacon, frying it up in a pan, and taking care of the home, meals, and children plus all their activities is just too much for one person. There has never been a better time to make money online! Getting paid to live is working smarter, not harder. Find the things you love and are passionate about, and be authentic, unapologetic, and honest with yourself about what YOU really want out of life. We all have the same 24 hours in a day, so be intentional about how you spend it.

The truth is, you can't do anything you want to, you can do anything you believe you can do! I'm proof of that, coming from nothing, and in the last year made the decision to move our family to the beach where and HOW I have always dreamed of living. And I'm just getting started…

Expert Tips: Manifesting

- **Rule #1.** Be clear and concise! Get crystal clear on what you want (not on what you don't want). Where your focus goes, your energy flows! Anytime I catch myself thinking about what I do not want, I simply say aloud, "Thank you God for showing me that I am focusing on and creating what I do not want in my life. Thank you for redirecting my focus to gratitude."

- **Rule #2.** Visualize and hold the feeling for 17 seconds. One hour of visualization is equivalent to 2000 hours of man work! Get a picture, or visualize in your mind what it looks like, what it feels like, what people will say to you, and how you will feel when they say those words to you. Really FEEL it for at least 17 seconds!! And affirm it! Affirm at least twice daily, aloud!

- **Rule #3.** Have faith it is done and live from the wish fulfilled. You must have unwavering faith that it's done. Live and speak as if you already have what it is you desire. Give gratitude as if you have already received it. Match the frequency of the vibration you want; meaning, if you're low vibe and low energy, you will attract just that. Have more fun, joy, and laughter! Find ways to raise your vibration, and you will start attracting more fun, joy, and laughter, as well as more financial abundance and favor.

Mary Sorobey

CEO of Sorobey Psychology

Mary Sorobey is an addictions and self-empowerment expert. As a registered psychologist with the College of Alberta Psychologists and the Psychologists Association of Alberta, she holds a Master's degree in Counselling. She is the owner and founder of Sorobey Psychology Centre, her private psychology practice, and Sorobey Assessments, providing proactive workplace addictions assessments and education.

Mary believes in the power of hope and that each person is an expert in their own life. But sometimes, we need support to find our resilience and become empowered to make the changes and choices to move in a more positive direction.

She is a mom to two beautiful and adventurous daughters, married to her high school sweetheart, is a volunteer, and a passionate outdoorswoman. Mary continues her studies in addiction and is a certified Canadian Addictions Counselor. She lives in Edmonton, Alberta, Canada. You can get in touch with her by visiting www.SorobeyPsychology.com.

https://www.linkedin.com/in/mary-sorobey-88065b54/
https://www.facebook.com/Sorobey.Psychology.Centre/
www.sorobeypsychology.com
www.sorobeyassessments.com

DISCOVERING THE TIGER LILY, YOUR RESILIENT SPIRIT

By Mary Sorobey

I've been there. That place that tells you that you "can't," "shouldn't," and even if you do, "you will fail."

But here is what I want to ask you to do, even if it's just for this chapter of the *Purpose-Driven Paycheck*: shut that voice out of your head and heart. Then go one step further. Become a Tiger Lily. Because Tiger Lillies are survivors and thrivers.

They always find a way to bloom.

Dear reader, my name is Mary Sorobey, registered Psychologist. For the last 20+ years, I've been helping people face the voice that holds them back, create new and healthy ways of being, and overcome the addictions that fuel the sense of purposelessness in their lives. I'm also a mother, wife, and entrepreneur, running a private practice, AND a consultant to big businesses and treatment centers.

Sometimes, it's a lot.

All the time, it's my purpose.

I thrive on challenges AND the challenge of the unknown. And I do this because I've discovered the flower in my heart, a Tiger Lily. And I want you to find the flower in your heart, too.

Every Flower Starts as a Seed

It's funny how big moments in life often fly under the radar, and we only recognize them years later when we look back and connect the dots. For me, that big moment was a phone call.

When I was little, I wanted to be a teacher. I'd play "school" every day, lecturing my stuffed animals and dolls, and handing out pretend homework. And if you had asked little Mary what she wanted to be when she grew up, she'd have told you, all matter-of-fact, "I'm gonna be a teacher!"

I thought I had my future figured out. But then, in 8th grade, everything changed.

Back then, I had a friend who was having a hard time at home and struggling with low self-esteem—pretty common for middle schoolers, I know. It wasn't a mystery that he was having a hard time, but it turned out the situation was much worse than I thought. One day he called me, and I could tell that something was wrong. And then it came out—he was planning to jump off a bridge to end his life. I can still feel the sudden confusion and fear.

But for some reason, I didn't freak out.

I just talked. And talked. And we kept talking, unwinding the pain and hopelessness, until he finally said, "I'm not going to do it." Thankfully, he didn't jump that day. And I'm happy to share that over the years, I've bumped into him. He's a dad and husband now, and he's seemed happy when I've seen him.

That day, the seed was watered.

Instead of wanting to be a teacher, I decided to become a Psychologist. It was my calling. Just by talking (a skill that comes easily to me) to a friend in need, I realized I could help people take control of their lives. I could help them make better decisions and choose to keep living.

So, that's what I decided to do.

Reaching for the Sun

In my years as a psychologist, I've learned that connecting with people and seeking to understand them fills my heart and challenges my mind. Being able to look someone in the eyes and see their potential, pain, kindness, sadness, or happiness is one of the strongest skills I've got.

We've all got this ability to some extent, but we don't use it the same way.

When I'm working with people, I always follow my heart, my inner guidance. This has helped me stay humble and helped my clients feel comfortable. It's allowed them to open up, trust me, and be honest with themselves. Because in my personal and professional experience, healing often starts with honesty and vulnerability, and many people struggle to find a safe place to do that.

When you genuinely listen to and understand someone without any preconceived notions or stereotypes, it's an incredible feeling. A big part of my job involves following my heart and helping others feel secure enough to open theirs.

Have you ever taken a moment to think about the key moments in your life? Like really, truly reflected? I bet there's stuff your mind brings up that you brush off or try to forget. Maybe those times were tough, painful, or even hurtful. Or perhaps they were moments that your mind and heart wanted you to remember and learn from.

Our hearts and minds guide us, giving us little nudges in different directions. We get to decide how we react: to ignore the thought, explore it, or put it on hold and come back to it later. Our brains are unique. What my mind tells me to do, like follow my heart and help others, is different from someone else who might want to plan weddings, arrange vacations, or become a mechanic.

We're not supposed to squeeze into each other's expectations.

We're meant to follow our own journeys, guided by our own hearts and thoughts. So, what's something you think about exploring more deeply but are too scared to try?

When it comes down to it, I'm not sure "failure" is even a real thing, and if it is, it's the fertilizer of your growth.

Braving Wild Winds

Bud to Blossom

Like a Wild Tiger Lily, resilience is a strength that has shown up again and again on my career path.

I began my journey by working with children in various environments: group homes, foster care, and schools. A door swung open when I took a job as a family counselor, which unexpectedly led me into the field of addictions.

Despite my lack of professional experience in this area, I refused to let anxiety beat me. I accepted the challenge and immersed myself in designing programs, running parenting groups, and working within a treatment center. Just as the Tiger Lily stands tall in harsh conditions, my passion for helping those battling addiction grew on this unexpected path.

The fear of judgment or perceived shortcomings might have hindered me. Still, I understood the importance of stepping into the unfamiliar, of learning and growing in the face of discomfort. Embracing my vulnerabilities, I strove to turn "I can't" into "watch me."

Wind And Drought

My petals opened to full bloom when I made the (terrifying) decision to leave the comfort of my secure government job. I wanted more autonomy, to make my own path, even if it meant stepping into uncertainty once again.

I traded stability for the chance to create a schedule that suited me and my family. Despite doubts, fears, and the lack of a cheerleading squad, I leaned into my heart's whisper to leap. I weathered storms, with my bank account dwindling to $5 at times.

Yet I stood firm against the wind of change, the financial drought, and the urge to quit.

The Delicate Balance

Each Flower is Perfect in its Season

During that period of change and growth, I started focusing more on my health and wellness. Because I knew that if I wanted to keep growing, I had to nurture my body and mind.

This new focus opened up fresh opportunities for me. Slowly, I began coaching a small group of women on health, wellness, emotional wellbeing, empowerment, and self-esteem. Seeing women supporting other women to become stronger, braver, and to forge their businesses and paths was deeply fulfilling.

At first, this coaching felt like abandoning my original vision and goals. It was like setting foot on a new path that I wasn't sure would lead me back to my initial journey.

But reflecting back, I realize it was a detour of personal growth. It helped me step out of my shell more fully, embrace vulnerability, take risks, and grow professionally and personally.

Health and wellness coaching was a crucial turning point, allowing me to be more genuine and establish connections I'd never imagined.

Another petal in my heart unfolded.

But this new phase had challenges. Juggling all of my various roles was a constant struggle. And I soon figured out I couldn't simultaneously be a wellness coach, support my private Psychology practice, meet my family's needs, and stay connected to myself.

Every person's energy has its limits, and my relentless drive to excel in every new venture was becoming exhausting. This truth hit me hard.

Anxiety and high-functioning stress were my constant companions, and the thought of needing to give something up created a subtle and growing sense of inadequacy.

But then, one day, a client—because I always learn from my clients—shared her story and strategy. She told me that focusing on one area of her life at a time helped her better understand and manage the changes she had to make. This seed of wisdom became a major turning point for me.

If you strive to be everything to everyone, you will burn out. However, by choosing to be deliberate and focused, you will have the energy to pursue the path that is most important to you.

Rocky Soil

Of course, there will always be obstacles, both inside and out. There will be naysayers and haters projecting their perceptions of your impending 'failure.' But your dreams and passions are independent of them—it's not about their acceptance, approval, or choices.

Your journey is uniquely and exclusively yours.

If you're an entrepreneur like me, internally, the biggest hurdle you'll likely face is the 'perfection' trap. The term 'perfection' is misleading. From an early age, we (women especially) are conditioned to conform to societal standards. Even though the world is beginning to recognize women's entrepreneurial skills, the societal expectation to excel as a mother, partner, and homemaker persists.

This can feel like a never-ending tornado. But it's crucial to stop and breathe. There is no 'perfect,' and there is no final destination. And if you are like me, I want you to start questioning what 'perfect' means. Would you know if you've reached this elusive 'perfection'? Or would 'perfect' just change its shape to meet a different set of unrealistic demands?

Defining success and setting goals while focusing on clear behaviors and outcomes can guide your journey. It helps you to concentrate on what's important to you, not what others perceive as important.

Watering Your Roots

When you're building your business or expanding your dreams, don't forget the most crucial part of the journey–YOU.

Building your dream and passion requires energy, stamina, and resilience. And if you ignore your own needs and don't invest time in self-care, you'll eventually run out of the energy you need to keep pursuing your dream.

Self-care is the root of a balanced life, emotional wellness, and the enduring strength to continue your journey, and it's essential to find ways to replenish your resources. This replenishment can come from a walk outside, quality time with a friend, a relaxing bath, reading a book, doing yoga, exercising, taking a nap—whatever works for you.

The key is to be aware of your feelings. Perform daily check-ins or do a body scan. Ask yourself, "How am I feeling?" "What does my body feel like?" "Is there tension in my body?" "Am I more irritable, tired, or angry?"

If the answer to any of these is yes, you're not refilling your energy reserves. I often use this analogy: you wouldn't embark on a road trip with your car's gas tank empty. Similarly, ensure your tank is full before you begin your daily journey.

Always remember to be kind to yourself and allow time for breaks. Water the seed of your resilience.

The Tiger Lily Unfolds

One Petal at a Time

Like a Tiger Lily weathering life's storms and droughts, I've continued to grow. But I don't have anything that you don't.

What's gotten me to where I am and what will see me into the future is staying true to myself: compassion, empathy, and a judgment-free spirit. I can't change others but can guide them to ignite their inner light and see the root of self-doubt, anxiety, and fear.

I allow myself to be inspired by the people I serve, people who have battled serious addictions and have experienced VERY tough times. Their sacrifices to overcome challenges, protect their families, and save themselves are the mirror against which I see my struggles and strength.

Who inspires you?

Growing in Uncertainty

Visualize yourself as the Tiger Lily ready to bloom, and confront your fear. When doubt paralyzes you, feel your roots drawing life from your purpose, the pursuit or passion that nurtures your spirit. However you've dealt with self-doubt and fear in the past, give yourself permission to show up and GROW.

Strive to be present, genuine, and patient with yourself, embodying the Tiger Lily's resilience no matter the storm and drought.

Reflecting on my 22-year journey, I see the Tiger Lily's path to growth in my own — from the vulnerability of a bud to the resilience of a full bloom. My work doesn't change people; it supports them while they courageously change themselves.

Our paths sometimes have fear and uncertainty, but I encourage you to listen to your inner call. Use your fear as fuel to propel you forward. Embrace the discomfort, take risks, and reveal the resilient Tiger Lily within you. There's no failure in trying. After all, even the most magnificent orange and black Tiger Lily begins as a vulnerable bud, taking a leap of faith into full blossom.

Embrace your journey and fearlessly unfold your petals, one at a time, to reveal your unique bloom. Trust the process, open your heart, and let the universe guide you. The result will be a beautiful, resilient blossom that was worth the risk.

Conclusion: You Bloom

Your dream is yours and to pursue your passion is a blessing. And while not everyone will understand or endorse it, your purpose-driven paycheck allows you to live intentionally.

Your dream is your unique gift and legacy. Will you let it slip away or watch others realize their dreams while you give in to fear? Or will you seize the opportunities life offers and actualize your vision?

If you doubt your ability to succeed, to open that business, to accept that promotion, to take risks, remember to be open to opportunities and follow your heart. Somewhere, someone is waiting for you to live your dream, inspiring them to do the same.

Challenges are inevitable, but they can be what waters your resilient spirit.

Don't surrender to the voices saying "can't" and "shouldn't," or try to predict failure. You're a Tiger Lily blooming amidst life's challenges and very normal self-doubt. Despite the hardship and times of drought, you bloom time and time again.

You can discover your resilient spirit, just like the Tiger Lily.

Expert Tips:

Creating Resiliency On Your Path To A Fulfilling Career

- Don't let fear hold you back—you have a purpose, and it's important that you find it.

- Listen to your gut—if you are thinking of something or want to try something new, there is probably a reason. My brain and heart don't tell me to open a mechanic shop, to search out antiques and sell them, or open a cleaning company—BUT yours might.

- Self-care is the backbone of a balanced life and emotional wellness. This can be a walk outside, a good time with a friend, a bath, reading a book, yoga, exercise, or napping.

- Be humble, be kind, be open to being a beginner (no matter where you are in your career/life).

- Take the open doors. Even if it doesn't work out, you will always gain something. There is no loss in trying and no such thing as 'failure.'

- Make connections. Not just at networking events BUT everywhere. Your kickboxing partner may just be a connection to an amazing opportunity.

- Drop the perfectionism! Being able to define success and goals and focus on tangible behaviors and outcomes helps you focus on what is important, not what you think others think is important.

Jacqueline Long, MA, MPA, MS

Founder of Elevate Your Biz Coaching and Consulting

Jacqueline is a Business Marketing Strategist, Podcast Host, and Master Certified Transformation & Mindset Coach.

She helps women start and scale coaching businesses online. She is the Founder of Elevate Your Biz Coaching and Consulting, LLC—her official brand dedicated to women up-leveling in life and business.

Jacqueline has three graduate degrees (a Master of Public Administration, MS in Human Resources Management & MA in Criminal Justice). Prior to starting her coaching business, she had a 22-year career in the non-profit & private sectors. She has served as a Director of Case Management, Director of Social Services, Director of AIDS Clinical Trials, and Vice President of Human Resources.

Jacqueline is a native New Yorker and first generation American. Her family is from the beautiful twin Caribbean islands of Trinidad and Tobago. She enjoys music, traveling, reading, and studying cultures & languages. She has two daughters and lives in the Atlanta Metro area.

Currently, Jacqueline is writing her first book and working on her PhD in Education.

www.facebook.com/JacquelineLongElevateYourBizOfficialPage/
https://www.facebook.com/groups/elevatedfemaleentrepreneur/
https://www.facebook.com/groups/sheselevatingnowpodcastinggroup
www.elevateyourbizcoaching.com

SO, YOU WANT TO START A BUSINESS. REALLY?

By Jacqueline Long, MA, MPA, MS

"Great businesswomen are like diamonds: bright, rare, valuable, and always in demand."
—Jacqueline Long, MA, MPA, MS

Why would a woman of your experience, education, and skill want to start a business?

Don't you know how many businesses fail within the first year of starting?

I can't tell you how many times I was asked those questions when I decided to start my business. People are not afraid to hide their cynicism. But it didn't bother me because I don't live by what people think. I'm an overachiever, who marches to the beat of my own drum. Tell me I can't do something, and I'm going to do it. I don't follow the conventional rules for living life and achieving success. I've learned to do what feels best for ME.

If I had listened to the people who told me I would fail in business, I wouldn't have accomplished all that I have over the last several years. Today, I'm proud to say, I've created a profitable business; I'm traveling the world; I've visited my dream destination, Dubai; I've worked with amazing clients; I've met other interesting and accomplished 6- and 7-figure female entrepreneurs, including some of the co-authors of this book; I've created my own products, written my own courses, started my own podcast, and now co-authored a book. But how did I get here? Before I go on, let me share a little about myself and my journey.

Scared to Death

I started my online coaching business eight years ago. But first, I had a long career in the not-for-profit sector and held several positions: Director of Social Services, Director of Case Management, and Vice-President of Human Resources. I enjoyed coaching, supervising, managing, and hiring people. I also enjoyed managing budgets and departments. But after many years, I felt burnt out and frustrated. You see, I did everything "right." You know, the way we were taught to traditionally—go to college, get a good job, work for many years, earn a good pension, then retire. I graduated from college, earned three graduate degrees, worked hard, moved up to senior management and made a great salary. However, after working my way up the career ladder, I was jaded. I was tired of working long hours and spending less time with my family. I was displeased with management politics, nepotism, and staff turnover. I was bored with projects I had no interest in and unhappy with 3% annual raises. But I was especially frustrated with budget constraints and the C-suite wanting MORE from employees, for less. At times, I absolutely hated waking up to go to work. I was over it all. It was time for a change. I started to think, "I want to start my own business." But it felt unrealistic. And it was risky and scary. I HAD to work; I had bills, student loans, and a family to support. How could I?

A Life Changing Decision…

Walking away from my career, an excellent salary, and benefits, was foolish. That's what I was told repeatedly. But, after many years of managing other people's businesses, I was ready.

I had learned a lot and it was time to pursue my own dream. But whenever I talked about wanting to start my own business, I heard many discouraging things, like, "Really?" "You're crazy," and "That's dumb." When I made the decision, I had to give some people in my life the pink slip. They were either with me, or they weren't. It was going to be a long and tough road ahead and I had my own negative self-talk to deal with. I didn't need that additional negativity or noise in my head. In 2013, I made a life changing decision. I left my job, moved my family to Georgia, and started a new life. Two years later, I would build a profitable brand and business. Fast forward, here I am today, a full-time entrepreneur, living a laptop lifestyle, with no regrets.

That's how it started for me. It has been amazing, and I've had many successes. But it hasn't been all "diamonds and rosé." I struggled at times. I've had challenges and setbacks that made me question my decisions and sanity. There were times that I didn't achieve my revenue goals, had failed launches and doubted myself at every step. In the middle of it all, I was also managing my personal life. I was raising two girls and caring for my elderly mother. In 2018,

I was hit by a car and needed months of therapy to recover from my injuries. I bounced back, continued working with clients, and started my PhD in Education, only to then lose my mother, my rock. It was tough! But I was determined. I learned one important thing about business and life: failures and setbacks are part of the process. They are never permanent unless you allow them to be.

You may be thinking, *But Jacqueline, what did you do to get started and have a thriving business now?* Well... first I assessed what I was good at and what kind of business I wanted to start. With my professional work experience, coaching people, leading, and marketing came naturally to me. I decided that business coaching was the perfect match. I leveraged the many skills I had acquired over the years in research, business, leadership, and finance, and put them all to work. My formal education played an important role in my success, given that I had the writing and research skills that enabled me to create my programs and marketing strategy.

In May of 2015, I hired my first business coach to help build the foundation of my business and master my online marketing. I needed the support to learn how to think like an entrepreneur and manage being my own boss. I learned important things from my coach, like what I wanted, who I wanted to help, how to manage my business and how I needed to grow. I took what I learned from my coach and tweaked it, to create a business strategy and plan that was best for me and my business. I worked with my coach for six months and learned all the ins and outs of marketing and sales, online coaching, and consulting. She was a master at it. The investment in working with her was substantial, but invaluable. She helped me to build a business and mindset for entrepreneurial success. Without her expertise and encouragement, I don't know that I would have made it this far. Like many entrepreneurs who start businesses, I might have given up at the first failure or sign of struggle. But I didn't because... I learned from the best.

I would make many more investments in coaching, masterminds, courses, conferences, memberships, books, and small products to grow and expand my business annually. I even hired coaches to help me manage my finances and fears and doubts when things got tough. With their support, I would build a brand that enabled me to serve clients and make money doing what I enjoy. I learned, created, implemented, invested, and marketed my services. Today, I impart what I have learned to my clients.

A Final Word

I shared my story in the hope that it will inspire you in some small way. However, here's what I really want you to know—while there have been challenges along the way, starting a business is doable. Entrepreneurship can be fun and rewarding. But it's not for everyone. Only the toughest and smartest survive. However, if you choose this path, the opportunities are endless, and the connections are invaluable. With the right support, belief in yourself, and unwavering commitment, building a business and realizing this dream is possible for you. Therefore, if this is what you truly desire, get started now. I share some expert tips and recommendations to help you get started below.

Finally, starting a business is uncomfortable and scary. But you'll learn a lot and experience the rewards of your hard work in the end. There will be successes, mistakes, bad investments, failures, and hardships. But it's all part of the process and it will strengthen you. Start now, expect the unexpected, embrace the process and enjoy the journey. I wish you the best.

Elevate!

Expert Tips: How to Jumpstart Your Business and Avoid New Entrepreneur Mistakes

Over the years, I've worked with new entrepreneurs and observed their struggles and mistakes. Therefore, I'm sharing the following tips and words of wisdom to support you in getting started successfully and avoiding some of the common new entrepreneur pitfalls:

- *Get Support* – Surround yourself with like-minded people. Develop relationships with other entrepreneurs. They can be a great source of advice and support. Discuss your business with people who love and support you. One of the major things that impedes entrepreneur success is non-supportive people. As an entrepreneur, you're going to face challenges and negative self-talk of your own. You don't need other negative voices in your head. Surround yourself with people who will be your guides and cheerleaders.

- *Mindset & Confidence* – You can't become an entrepreneur with a 9 to 5 employee mindset, lack of belief in yourself or lack of confidence. Entrepreneurship requires developing positive thoughts, beliefs, and confidence in large doses. You must thicken your skin and nurture your confidence and mindset consistently. Develop a daily practice of reading to build your wealth consciousness, expertise, and mind. Make this a mandatory part of your daily routine. An example of my daily mindset routine includes: journaling, practicing gratitude, reading self-development, wealth, and success books, and repeating positive affirmations that help me to counter the sneaky, negative self-doubt and words that enter my thoughts occasionally. Develop a winning mindset and never accept failure as an option.

- *Self-Development* — Be coachable and open to learning and investing in yourself. You can't be successful in business without investing in the skills, knowledge, and support needed to grow. I've spoken to many aspiring, new, and scaling entrepreneurs and the difference between very successful entrepreneurs and those who struggle or give up is their willingness to invest, learn, and evolve. Successful entrepreneurs are constantly learning and developing their knowledge and expertise. Take steps to grow and elevate yourself and your biz consistently.

- *Build Your Business Foundation* – Get clarity first. Some questions to ask yourself: Why are you starting this business? What kind of business are you starting? Who is the ideal client for your business? How will you find your clients? What do you need to get started? What will you offer? What is your marketing and sales plan? Do some market research to start. Interview your target market/ideal clients. Consult with a business attorney. Get your policies, procedures, and contracts in place. Research how to register your business within your country, state, or municipality. Determine what systems you need, such as how you'll receive payments, how you'll deliver your product/services, what tools or platforms you'll need to market and sell. A successful business starts with getting clarity and building your foundation. This is an important step. Do not skip it.

- *Marketing Strategy* - If you're not an expert at marketing/sales, hire a marketing strategist or business coach to teach you how. A business coach will be your mentor and support for questions, business advice, and strategy. New entrepreneurs come to me all the time with websites and every single social media platform set up, but no sales, leads, or clients. They say, "I'm struggling, Jacqueline. How do I get clients and make sales?" And I explain, you're struggling because there are gaps in your foundation, and you have no marketing/sales strategy. Your business MUST have a marketing and sales strategy to sell and make money. People are not going to buy just because you have a website or business social media profiles. You must have a strategy. Therefore, get marketing/sales support. Your business and success depend on it.

Teri Nolan

Energy Grid Technology Leader

Teri is a strategic leader in the energy-utility sector, focusing on US grid efficiency programs, electric vehicles, and smart-cities development. Teri lives with her family in the Charlotte, NC area.

Teri has always been driven toward civic leadership and urban infrastructure, but also had a strong desire to devote herself fully to motherhood when her children were young. She chose to leave her early corporate sales career to become a stay at home mother and finish her college studies. While in her forties, Teri earned a bachelor's degree in International Relations and Environmental Sustainability, from Harvard University.

Since then, Teri has launched a fast-moving career working in Smart Cities development, Energy Resources, EV, and enjoys speaking at regional and national energy industry events.

https://terinolan.blogspot.com/

GOVERNING YOUR LIFE WITH FIERCE DETERMINATION

By Teri Nolan

When asked to write a chapter on my road to success, I imagined how fun it would be. But I quickly discovered how difficult it can be to pinpoint the exact moment of transformation. Often it is a convoluted process of actions mixed with painful emotions and the things that propel us to grow, to do more, to be better, are frequently a result of overcoming tough circumstances. Though I do believe that in telling one's story it is important to be specific about the key events that are recognizable catalysts to change. In my case, I recognize that the most painful parts of my past were the times when the best foundations for growth were being laid, and so despite some anxiety around them, I feel compelled to reveal those stories.

Growing up in the Nolan house with two young parents and four young kids, it was filled with love, but not much else. With parents barely making ends meet, we learned to work for our existence. Everyone pitched in and with four girls (and no boys) we learned to work hard. Dad was an engineer, earning his license while working, and Mom worked at car dealerships where she sold and then ran financial departments. In hindsight, our life was not that hard, but we complained about having little and needing to pitch in, especially when Dad made us shovel snow—which in Michigan in the 1980s meant A LOT of snow. Sometimes, we had to pick ice at the end of the driveway while the other kids made fun of us, and the neighbors shook their heads to say what a shame that we had to work so hard. Of course, we had NO idea that Dad was trying to train us for adulthood until much later. He wanted us to learn how to do hard things, to push ourselves to the limits, learn responsibility, and believe in ourselves.

I was a straight A student, but apparently even smart girls can make dumb choices if they are careless, especially where boys are concerned.

During high school, my big lofty dreams turned to dust, thanks to lack of planning—and the fact that I was too caught up with Mr. McDreamy, who had his own ambitions that did not include me. So, while my friends went to great colleges and lived in fancy dorms, I went to a local state college and was bored to tears. Ultimately, I dropped out, took a job, and married a boy, mainly because everyone else was doing it and because I lacked forward vision.

Predictably, three years and one baby later, I found myself at the age of 25, divorced, broke, uneducated, stressed, and terrified. My parents still had teenagers at home, so I had to figure it out on my own with very little support. They were NOT happy with me, and I don't blame them. But, I knew I was in the wrong situation and was desperately trying to find a path that felt right. The problem was that I didn't know who I was. I didn't know what I liked, or didn't like, what I believed in, or why my life mattered. I had to learn and had to be tough—so I found an apartment, and a $9 per hour job and started over with a baby in tow.

In the early days, I was run-down, exhausted, and distraught, as a number of fears would often overtake me. There were nights where I sobbed and shook so hard that I would become breathless and pass out on the floor. I would awaken in the middle of the night terrorized by what would become of my son and me. I couldn't see past the end of the week- let alone the rest of my life. However, over the next few years, my relationship and belief in God would become the most important factor in my healing and success. Chasing Him-and his principles- is the thing that I am certain catapulted me from the depths of despair into the realm of the living. I now say, "sometimes you get so low, you have nowhere else to look but up!" I began to spend my weekdays working and my weekends either parenting or reading. I had zero interest in partying, but because of this adversity I had developed a huge interest in and intense focus on building my own future life.

I began to read the Bible and go to Church regularly, which really helped with my prayer life, and I could begin to see the light at the end of the dark tunnel. Thanks to the life training from Dad, I was tough enough to endure the harshness of that life and pull myself up by my big-girl bootstraps. But (and this is one thing I like about myself), once I believe in something, I am committed and fiercely determined. This attribute became imperative to my success, as not only do we ASK God for what we need, we must also be DETERMINED (faith-filled) that it will happen. So, I began to SPEAK and COMMAND the things I wanted and I worked hard for them...the new rental house by the playground so my boy could play on the swing set! Then, I asked for the promotion at work, the new company-paid car, the expense account! My faith grew and I worked harder and dreamed bigger, becoming more confident with each victory. I was blessed with opportunities that seemed to fall from the sky—the phone ringing to deliver the new opportunities I wanted! I wanted to own my own house, so I went and bought one! The more I focused and wrote lists of my wants and expectations—and PRAYED over them—the more these prayers were answered and manifested...to the exact detail of my ask. It was uncanny, surreal, nearly unbelievable. I had been reading about prayer and manifestation and was amazed how they happened— and continue to happen—in my life.

When I later married my sweet husband—who also had been a dad and understood my single parenting life—I was in my early thirties and we agreed I would return to finish college, and possibly law school. Alas, life had its own plans and our love brought two more kids (!) and ten years later, I was still not back to school or a career. Although I was very grateful for the experience I had as a stay-at-home Mommy, wearing babies on my hip, growing gardens to make home-cooked meals; I loved cleaning my house with Martha Stewart tips and tricks— I even had her homemaking book! As the saying goes, "we didn't have much, but we had each other," although my personal dreams were again slipping away.

The annoyingly tight budget reminded me how I longed for success, and I missed the "Teri" who could have been. I was still there, somewhere, and I wanted education and success. But who would take me in my forties, and offer flexibility while offering worthwhile credentials? Returning to the workforce as a middle-aged woman is not the easiest thing to do. Employers often say they overlook the "Motherhood gap," but after seeking work for quite a long time, I beg to differ. I wasn't ready to settle for entry level admin, when I had already been a global sales rep. No way. I had a brain and grit. I knew it was going to be "go big, or go home," which meant getting good degree credentials. I tried to go back to the University of Michigan where I had taken some courses through the years, and many other colleges, but few had what I needed, and I was distraught.

In a dream one night, God said, "You're going to Harvard," and I said, "you're joking!" He wasn't. I was skeptical and did not feel worthy (that is a big understatement). I then discovered that Harvard had a bachelor's program that could be done hybrid—remote and on campus (who knew?) if you could pass three courses and get approved by the admissions board. Much to the shock of my parents and many others, I put my faith forward and three courses on a credit card. I told myself that I would try this—even if I were likely to fail. I shook in my shoes when I stood before NASA scientists and policy leaders in my first sustainability course, and I couldn't get the words past my closed-up throat in my first English Literature course! Ugh, how would I make it? But I tried anyway and a year later, I was accepted into the program—receiving a full scholarship with travel money to boot! Thanks, Harvard! I took student loans to pay our grocery bills and would spend the next four years doing the most intensive work— another understatement—of my life.

We had on-campus intensive requirements, and sometimes I brought my family with me to summer weeks, staying in cramped hotel rooms or rented houses. It was difficult but inspiring; I met the most amazing people, and my kids learned to experience a bit of the intellectual mecca that is Harvard. Eventually, I learned to stop shaking and speak freely, and that my brain hadn't completely lost all its cells. I learned what I liked, what I believed, and who I was, becoming solidly grounded within myself. I found that there is incredible strength in digging deep and learning your own truths.

In the end, I went from college drop-out, single mom, to graduating from Harvard with Honors and launched my second career in Energy Utility Technology. The rigorous training and high-demand performance matured me and grew me into a woman equipped with knowledge and steadfast confidence in my skill sets, and moreover, my life. On graduation day, my family and I stood fifty feet away from Mark Zuckerburg at the speaker's podium, where he received his honorary Doctorate (Hey, Mark, I had to do the work)!

Currently, I am six years into my new line of work where I contribute to Smart Cities, Electric Vehicles, and Distributed Energy programs. I sit on steering committees with Capitol Hill industry groups, speak on national platforms, and contribute to making the world a more efficient and resourceful place. I still have dreams of working in Congress, Energy Policy Lobby, or similar. But I am thoroughly enjoying myself at this time and will let life play out day by day. I may yet be the oldest law school student, but we shall see.

In hindsight, I know that sometimes life requires stepping stones and extreme commitment to achieve your dreams. It's ok to take those, but more importantly—and especially as women—we must fiercely govern our own lives, being thoughtful about our plans, and absolutely tenacious in our desires to achieve. Figure out who you are, and make her dreams come true!

Top 10 TIPS for Success:

1. Be firmly planted in your desires and asks. I learned to control my thoughts and internal dialogue. Once committed to something I want, I learned to refuse any doubtful or negative thoughts and feelings.

2. Learn to put love energy toward your thoughts. Energy comes from the heart chakra, which forces action in our third dimension—this sounds ethereal, but it's proven in scientific studies. If you operate from a place of love, you will experience rapid manifestations.

3. In reading books by Dr. Wayne Dyer on the power of intention, I learned to be very specific about each thing I needed and to be fiercely determined to receive it. I put it to the test repeatedly and it has always worked.

4. I could write an entire chapter on my faith journey alone, but let it be sufficient to say to any woman seeking success, stability, safety...seek your Father in Heaven first, and He will provide you with everything you need.

5. Practice daily affirmations and meditations. Within the first hour of each day, I set my intentions for the day, visualizing tasks and events and how I wish for them to go—positive and with good outcomes. Prayer helps me—I say the rosary a few times per week—and helps to draw universal goodness toward my intentions for myself and others.

6. Staying organized is important. I like systems for my home and business, to a large degree. I use shareable task lists, Trello management system, email-linked calendars. I teach my children to use their phone apps and lists, and to hold themselves accountable for their own activities—to varying

degrees. This gives me time back in my day, and teaches them responsibility and organizational skill sets: a win-win!

7. Plan your day. I do this at work and home and prioritize my activities based on the level of importance. I skip unimportant emails and allow critical issues to force their way to the surface. I do my own tasks first and let the phone calls and other disruptors wait, so I remain in control of my time and agenda.

8. Delegate where possible. I don't take on extra tasks or do more detailed work than necessary. I threw my tendency for perfectionism out the window. I try to keep my family on schedules and give task lists so that they can take some household burdens from me, as they also should be supporting our family while mom and dad work. It has great benefits for all of us.

9. Keep your home and work life in balance. This means staying organized at home—hire it done if needed. I keep my home fairly clear and orderly, as it makes me feel good to move and create in a clean space. I help and guide my children to organize their rooms and closets so they can also be free of clutter and chaos. We play easy music in the home, and try to keep the environment healthy and light. Home should be a respite for all—and it is a challenge with two businesses running in the same place we live.

10. Being successful requires a holistic approach, and we need to support our health. I focus heavily on nutrition for myself and family. We eat clean, fresh foods, mainly organic. We do health shakes, smoothies, filtered water, and constantly find new ways to add nutrients and tons of sunshine—at least an hour per day is mandatory—even in the winter.

Marco and Tiffany Conde

Founder of Prosper with Purpose Financial

Tiffany and Marco Conde just celebrated 15 years of marriage, raising four wonderful children ages 12 to 1 in South Florida. They love sports, cooking, making memories, fitness, and the ocean.

They are the proud owners of Prosper with Purpose Financial, headquartered in Doral, Florida and one of the biggest and fastest growing Life & Health Insurance Brokerages in the country. The company was built on faith, delivering a customized experience for every client, and the love for helping others.

Marco Conde is a first generation Cuban American while Tiffany Conde was born and raised in New Jersey. They both became licensed in the insurance industry in 2020 after Marco was unexpectedly laid off from Corporate America.

They are here to share their testimony in hopes of inspiring others. They believe with your eyes UP on God in all aspects of life, you can rise UP and prosper with purpose.

https://www.linkedin.com/company/prosper-with-purpose-financial
https://www.facebook.com/ProsperWithPurposeFinancial/
https://www.instagram.com/prosperwithpurposenow/
https://www.fflprosperwithpurpose.com

STRUGGLE LEADS TO STRENGTH

By Marco and Tiffany Conde

The power of God and living on purpose for a purpose.

I was there… the place I'd always dreamed of getting to. Twenty-plus years in Corporate America: I had climbed the corporate ladder; poured everything I had into leading large projects; managed teams internationally in the telecom/tech space; spent most weeks on a plane traveling to different states away from my wife and children. All of that hard work led me to the cusp of the position I most coveted: Vice President. Everything was falling into place, as it truly felt like the culmination of the many sacrifices my family and I had made during this long period of time. And then it happened… the unexpected announcement of a newly hired Chief Revenue Officer. Despite being told my position was secure and that my running for the Vice President role was intact, I was laid off a couple of months later. I had just traveled to meet with my team and celebrate my region's number one finish for the previous quarter. What a great accomplishment! Well, we all know with highs come lows, and this is when I was knocked to my knees. I was fired the very next day. I no longer felt like a person, just another statistic that got swallowed up by Corporate America. What was I going to tell my wife? How could I look my children in the eyes? Imagine being on a treadmill, running at full speed on an incline, and you're about to finish the best workout of your life. Then BAM! You trip over your laces and go flying into mid-air. The embarrassment, disbelief, pain, anger, fear, confusion…it would all set in fast. This is how I felt after being let go. In shock, I drove across the street of the hotel I was staying at, gathered my thoughts the best I could, called my wife Tiffany to break the news. I remember this day very clearly. She was with our little ones and they were out eating tacos. Right away she knew there was something wrong by the tone of my voice, so she excused herself from the table. The emotions and tears poured out. She tried to support me the best she could, telling me that it was okay and that we would make it work. I actually think she felt a sense of relief, as she long felt I was working tirelessly for a company and I wasn't home enough for myself, her, or our children. Our marriage suffered; our finances suffered; and there was indeed a disconnect at times. Although I felt like a failure, she had a sense of relief. She knew God had us in the palm of His hands and helped me see that I just was lost in my thoughts, unable to see that this was a blessing in disguise. Maybe, just maybe, this event could be what propels my family and I into a life-changing journey for the better. God knew exactly what He was doing. Sometimes our lowest points and hardships have to happen. God needed to move us, because we weren't going to do it willingly and that is the truth.

I flew home later that day to South Florida from North Carolina, officially unemployed. I felt like a big failure, one that let a lot of people down. At the time, I was the sole provider for Tiffany (who was previously an educator) and our three small children (we now have four). I had to turn in my company car, all of my company credit cards and equipment, and wrap my head around beginning a new job search. It was a lot to take on, but that is when God began showing me his plan. It felt as if I was being held under water and couldn't breathe. Did you ever feel like you just needed to breathe? Overwhelmed by the fear of the unknown? So many "what-ifs" circled through my thoughts. A few weeks prior to being laid off, a good friend of mine had invited me to a meeting for a business opportunity in the insurance industry. At that time, I politely replied that I was not interested, as I simply didn't have the time to consider adding a side gig. Fast forward to the day I lost my job, that same friend happens to reach out once again stating that the meeting he mentioned to me previously was coming up in a few days. We had also been told about the insurance industry by someone in our family and a friend of theirs. God was starting to clearly point us in a new direction, but we weren't listening. My wife finally came to me and said, "I feel like God is hitting us at all angles with this and we are not listening." To which I replied, "What if we lose everything?" She told me that we have to take the risk, and that she would fully support the risk, but would not support me taking another corporate job. That stung a bit, but she was right. Wow, I felt my back against the wall, scared and desperate. Tiffany and I made the decision to attend and hear about the opportunity; we went in very skeptical of everything.

Keep in mind, we knew nothing about the insurance industry, and we mean nothing, nada, zilch. At that time, if I closed my eyes and envisioned someone in the insurance industry, I pictured a disheveled, middle-aged man, wearing suspenders, carrying a briefcase, all while smoking a pack of cigarettes a day. Working long hours, cold-calling and harassing everyone they knew, including friends and family, and doing all of this for very little pay. So as open minded as I tried to be entering this meeting, my preconceived notions were strongly in place. Sitting in on that meeting, our first impression was that we were introduced to some amazing, God-fearing individuals... and the business opportunity laid out in the meeting honestly seemed too good to be true. My wife and I asked so many questions and just didn't believe how amazing it was. After a few hours, Tiffany and I went home, prayed about it, tried to figure out what the catch was (if there was any), and we researched everything we could regarding the insurance industry. What we came to find was that the business opportunity covered in the meeting was indeed one of the best in the industry. I still remember this day very clearly. The sun was shining into our kitchen. Not sure where our kids were at the moment, but she and I sat on the floor, backs against our kitchen island, side by side. We discussed what would happen if we did do it, if we didn't do it, our finances, our children, pros and cons of moving, maybe even moving in with our parents. Quick side note: This brought us so much closer. We became a team, we worked together, prayed together, leaned on one another, and it helped align our priorities. Not only did it save our family, it helped our marriage. So Tiffany and I decided to get our insurance licenses. We decided to go all in, studied every single day and passed our pre-licensing course followed by our state exam. Although I went all in, my inner perspective was that this would be a good side gig opportunity to have, just in case, while I looked for a "real job." I needed to have that weekly income, I needed the security. You know that saying…You make plans and God laughs. He walked with us the entire time, knowing that this was the beginning of a purposeful journey, where we would not only be changing the lives of our family but the families we worked with, protected and served. Not to mention, the brokers we would partner with.

Fast forward once again a few months later to January 2020, Tiffany and I are both licensed and contracted to sell life/health insurance. I had two telecom/tech director job offers in different parts of the country, and we had to make a critical decision at that very moment as our savings were depleted and my severance pay was running out. As I had mentioned previously, I will never forget Tiffany telling me that she would follow and support me no matter what, as long as I went into business for myself. At that moment, she believed in me more than I did and her unwavering faith brought peace to our family despite all of the turmoil. It was like a glimmer of light was shined over us, lighting up the pathway as we walked down a dark, unknown path. Your spouse's support can really impact the family, finances, and future decisions. Communication is key and not to be taken lightly. I made a promise to her and our children that I was never going to let another company, nor individual, ever control our family's financial security again. We had been burned, hurt, and thrown away as if we had no value, or so we felt. We also did not want to move and uproot our family, as stability was important for our kids, as they were at young tender ages. So we chose to spend our mortgage money for that month to buy insurance leads and jump into selling life insurance full time. We had nothing left, our money was gone. This was it! I have never been more scared in my life than at that very moment, as I knew no one in the insurance industry nor had I ever had any experience selling insurance. It was the complete unknown, but I just felt that God had placed us there for a reason, and we had to trust the holy spirit that was working inside of us.

So we went all in, I purchased the insurance leads, and Tiffany helped with calling and booking up my schedule with appointments for the first few months until I got my footing. We were focused, we had color-coded notes everywhere and kept learning as the curve balls were thrown our way. You know what? As humble as I thought I was, I quickly realized that I needed more humility than ever before. I went from being a well-known and respected senior leader in the telecom/tech industry, with a proven track record of performance, to being an independent insurance broker with zero knowledge, connections, or experience. A month after we started, the company we decided to partner with (Family First Life) was holding their annual convention in Las Vegas, and my wife and I knew that I had to find a way to attend no matter what, although we could not afford it. I had to swallow my pride and had to ask my mother-in-law if I could borrow her airline points and I used my hotel points to attend all three days. I had a fixed daily food budget, so I never once ate at a restaurant or went sightseeing around the city; no partying, no wasted time, money or energy; I completely focused and became a sponge to soak everything in. I spent every minute studying, learning, and boosting my belief system. I heard some incredible speakers, such as Pastor Matthew, who truly inspired and motivated me. I knew we were on the right track. We could do this. Would it be easy? No. Worth it? Yes. Best decision we ever made. Thank you God for making us so uncomfortable that we had to push through the suck.

Being new to the industry, we were forced to trust the process laid out for us. At first, I felt like I could take shortcuts because of my self-assumed skillset (AKA overconfidence) and the fact that I watched literally every training video/podcast available. I quickly was met with a rude awakening, as I realized that if you don't trust and execute ALL of the process, especially the parts you don't like or want to do, it simply won't work. That's the secret sauce—putting the numbers in my favor with leads, 8am dialing start time, truly resolving every lead, booking up my calendar with extra appointments, working on the weekends when others weren't to get ahead, etc. Once I began trusting and executing all of the process, the game changed for our business. We became obsessed with the process, following it with an unwavering level of discipline which led me to write over a million dollars of issue paid life insurance business in my first eighteen months, winning Rookie of the Year in 2020 and earning Hall of Fame recognition.

Since then, we have become maniacal about teaching others (in the industry or not) the exact formula behind our success, and sharing this life changing opportunity with the world. We have poured everything back into our business with passion and wisdom; we purchased and remodeled a beautiful office in Miami, Florida; hired an amazing staff; built a proprietary system where brokers and insurance agencies from across the country partner with us to successfully sell life/health/supplemental insurance. Prosper with Purpose Financial is now one of the biggest and fastest-growing independent insurance brokerages in the United States, helping over 5,000 families monthly. To say this journey has been life changing would be an understatement.

When your back is against the wall and you burn all of your boats, desperation sets in. Will you react or respond? Maybe both?

Communication will be key, and support from your spouse and/or family will be a very big contributing factor to your success. With your eyes up you too can RISE UP. Will it be hard? Yes! Will it be easy? NO. But you can do HARD THINGS my friend. No one said the path should or would be linear or easy, yet we often think it should be. Just imagine the line of your heartbeat on the monitor at the doctor's office, where you see continuous ups and downs. The same can be said about your journey, your path of life. There will be a lot of climbing back up, but that is what makes it that much sweeter at the very top. We are meant to help and inspire others as we climb. And *WHEN* (not if) you get to the top, remember you must work even harder to stay there because what is given to you can easily be taken away (so we have learned). Maybe you are unsure of your purpose, or maybe your purpose is to inspire others by sharing your story; maybe it is to raise good humans, or to lead others. Whatever it is, you were made for a PURPOSE on PURPOSE. What you think is your endgame is just another stepping stone, toning your muscles and preparing you for the fight that lies ahead. Keep going, take the risk and go all in with your eyes up on Him. Never forget that your lowest point might indeed be the best gift you didn't see coming. Remember that what is breaking you is also building you. In your toughest and most painful moments, God is working behind the scenes for a purpose. Lean all the way in, He's faithful always in all ways.

Elizabeth LeConey

Elizabeth LeConey Coaching & Creation
Business Strategy Coach

Elizabeth LeConey has been an accomplished entrepreneur for more than a decade, known for her expertise in Business, Leadership, and Branding Strategy. Her Equipped Entrepreneur Podcast is among the top 10% of global entrepreneurship podcasts. Elizabeth dove into entrepreneurship in 2012 when she launched a photography business and then two years later joined a network marketing company. After generating over one million dollars in her network marketing business, Elizabeth chose to step away from the industry due to health issues and burnout. She realized that she was not living in line with her strengths, holding onto outdated practices, and settling for a business that no longer inspired her. In search of a new direction, she launched her own coaching business, where today as a Business Strategist, she collaborates with driven entrepreneurs to help them build businesses that align with their passion and leverage their distinct talents.

https://www.facebook.com/elizabeth.u.leconey/
https://www.instagram.com/elizabethleconey/
www.elizabethleconey.com

BRAVELY PIVOT

By Elizabeth LeConey

I remember the moment clearly. I was sitting in my bedroom with tears running down my face wondering how in the world I got here. A place so polar opposite from where I started. Feelings of loneliness, confusion, and defeat were consuming me. My body was tired. My brain was tired. My family was tired. I knew that I had a decision to make. I could either continue down the path that felt safe and required little to no change, or I could pivot towards new beginnings. So in that moment, with a scared and defeated sigh, I chose, bravely, to pivot.

I knew at a young age that finding joy in what I do and using my natural skills and gifts were important to me. Having a corporate career for eleven years taught me that working for someone else, sitting in a cubicle, and accepting mediocrity was not something that I wanted. So, in 2014, I left my well-paying, "safe career" for my network marketing business. Heads turned, onlookers talked, and my parents were terrified. But I marched straight towards the dream of working for myself and doing what I loved with a sea of cheerleaders rooting me on.

I went on to grow an incredible business for a decade, learning and embracing new skills in leadership, marketing, public speaking, sales, and branding. For 10 years, this was my dream. I was living it. I lived, breathed, and was the face of my network marketing company.

And that was where I went wrong.

Looking back, it was in my seventh year when I started seeing signs that something in my life was off. But being the goal-oriented, hustling, workaholic that I was, I didn't notice them. It started with injuries, followed by anxiety, insomnia, and digestive issues. Over the course of two years, my health continued to decline. For a long time, I had no idea why, and neither did my doctors.

As I was forced to slow down, I started to notice that over the years I had distanced myself from my friends, family, and husband due to my relationship with work. I knew things weren't good, but I had become an expert in ignoring difficulties and seeking solace in the excitement of my growing business.

As time passed, I started questioning my career and direction. Had my love for this industry diminished from what it once was? Was this truly where I belonged? I tried to reassure myself that it was just a temporary phase. How could someone who had achieved my level of success not find happiness in their chosen profession? For a while, I believed that there was something fundamentally wrong with me. I convinced myself that consuming more podcasts, books, and training would reignite the passion I had left my corporate career for. However, as time went on, I came to the realization that not only was this approach futile, but I was also getting sicker. Everything seemed illogical. Anger, frustration, and loneliness overwhelmed me. I felt utterly lost.

I realized that I was pushing myself towards something that no longer suited me. I started recognizing the subtle signs my body had been trying to communicate to me for years, yet I had chosen to disregard. It became clear to me that my approach to work was completely out of sync with the rest of my life. I lacked proper boundaries, balance, and contentment, and unintentionally set a negative example for others. On the surface, I might have appeared successful, but deep down, I was filled with an internal turmoil that made me feel like an imposter.

I decided to take a professional pause and sought out mentorship. I took the year to focus on my health, figure out how I could start feeling better again, and find breathing room in my days to discover what I wanted. A few times, I thought I got really close to figuring it out. I now look at those attempts as necessary failures because while I didn't know it at the time, it would be the turning point for me in realizing exactly what I do want.

The coach I invested in at that time had a significant impact on shaping my current situation. Initially, when I was introduced to the idea of prioritizing flow over constantly striving for goals in business, I had doubts. I strongly held the belief that achieving desired outcomes demanded constant action, rather than slowing down.

My coach soon proved me wrong.

I came to realize that the reason I was struggling to heal was because I was hesitant to let go of certain burdens. My identity was closely tied to a career that no longer felt right for me. Instead of allowing myself to have faith in the journey, I was pushing myself excessively. Rather than fully embracing the here and now, I was constantly preoccupied with staying in motion.

It was time to pivot.

There's a grieving process that no one talks about much when you pivot from a career that you once loved. For me, it felt like a long break up where there was a lot of space, making up, trying to change, and blaming.

No one told me that pivoting could feel so messy—and lonely.

During those three years, I noticed many signs, but unfortunately, I couldn't admit that I had veered off course, even though it would have been better in a perfect world. That's just how life goes sometimes. I know I went through years of sickness, pain, and confusion, possibly so I can now help others spot these signs and guide them through their own struggles more easily.

As I look back on my past, I can clearly recognize four distinct stages that I went through. In addition, the more I talk to other women in the business world, the more I realize that these phases are common to many of us.

In the beginning, I was in the Unconscious phase, where my body gave me subtle hints that I failed to recognize as signs of burnout, lack of boundaries, and being out of alignment. I experienced symptoms like low energy, headaches, anxiety, digestive issues, and insomnia, but I didn't understand their significance. As I moved into the Conscious phase, I became aware that something was wrong and realized that my lack of healing was a result of not living in alignment with my true purpose. The Grief phase that followed was the most difficult for me, bringing feelings of frustration, loneliness, paralysis, and sorrow. It was challenging to accept and address the issue, especially because I had built my entire identity around my profession, which made the grieving process even more complicated. However, once I worked through this phase, I gained clarity and knew what actions I needed to take, leading me to the final Transformation/Evolution phase. This stage allowed me to pivot and embark on a new journey, utilizing the skills and talents I gained from network marketing to establish a coaching and design business. Reaching this point brought immense fulfillment as it allowed me to create a new identity and forge a path for myself by learning from past lessons and experiences.

This leads me to where I am today.

I consider myself incredibly fortunate to have the opportunity to serve as a guide for female entrepreneurs during their transformative pivot. It is a privilege to be able to support these remarkable individuals in developing a sense of clarity and strategy as they navigate through this crucial period of transition. My role is to help them create a business that not only aligns with their values and passions but also sets them up for long-term success.

Having embarked on this very same journey myself, I understand the complexities and challenges that can arise along the way. Therefore, I am here to provide unwavering support and guidance to others, ensuring they navigate their own path with heightened awareness and in a significantly shorter timeframe. It is my firm belief that each one of us is destined to pursue our dreams and reap the rewards that come from doing so. However, this often requires us to step out of our comfort zones, take calculated risks, and make pivotal changes in our chosen direction.

It is absolutely amazing to witness the multitude of exciting opportunities that lie beyond our fears and limitations. By taking that brave leap of faith and wholeheartedly embracing the entrepreneurial journey, we open ourselves up to a world filled with passion, purpose, and profitability. The possibilities are boundless for those who dare to chase their dreams and create something extraordinary.

So, to all the aspiring female entrepreneurs out there, I encourage you to cast aside any doubts or apprehensions that may be holding you back. Embrace the unknown, for it is within the realms of uncertainty that the most remarkable transformations occur. Together, let us embark on this empowering journey, where dreams become realities and success becomes second nature.

Expert tip on how to pivot/shift and start your passion-filled business:

- Your life has a cycle, a natural rhythm that indicates that staying in one place for an extended period is not the norm. It is essential to recognize and embrace this fact, as shifts and changes are not only inevitable but also beneficial for personal growth. Moreover, it is crucial to align your career objectives with this life cycle, ensuring that they adapt and evolve alongside you.

- To start, take the time to introspect and identify your passions and skills that can be monetized. Find that one gift or area where you thrive, your zone of genius. This is where your true potential lies and where you can excel. By understanding your strengths, you can create an irresistibly aligned offer that delivers a solution or transformation to your ideal client.

- Additionally, conduct a thorough market analysis of your profession, industry, and existing offers. This research will help you identify gaps in the market, areas where you can provide a unique perspective or approach. It is also an opportunity to establish your personal brand, differentiating yourself from competitors and positioning yourself as a standout professional.

- To ensure success, develop strategies, action steps, and processes that not only support your business but also keep you on track and aligned with your goals. These strategies can help you meet deadlines, improve the client flow experience, and simplify your workflow. By implementing efficient systems and taking proactive steps, you can optimize your productivity and achieve sustainable growth.

- Remember, your life is a continuous journey of evolution and change. Embrace the shifts, align your career objectives accordingly, and create a strong foundation for success by identifying your passions and strengths, offering unique solutions, and implementing effective strategies. Embracing the natural cycle of life and career will ultimately lead to personal fulfillment and professional accomplishment.

Colleen Paul-Hus

CEO of The PARC

Colleen Paul-Hus is the visionary, founder, and CEO of The Academy at the PARC, a practical arts educational resort campus in Sebring, FL. After feeling misalignment with traditional education, she and her husband, Rich, felt called to create an intentional educational environment where students could learn while surrounded by nature.

As a speaker, she has shared her insights at esteemed institutions such as The Huizenga College of Business and Entrepreneurship, Waldorf School of Palm Beach, and Education 2.0 Conference. She has been awarded the Humanitarian Award by Visit Sebring, Best Education Center in Sebring for two consecutive years, and the international Outstanding Leadership in Education award.

Colleen is most proud of raising their four children and for continuing to trust her intuition to make big and small decisions. Today, she continues to inspire and empower others to create unique learning environments that harmoniously integrate education, nature, nutrition, and emotional resiliency.

http://linkedin.com/in/colleen-paul-hus-8061a352
www.facebook.com/AcademyAtThePARC
www.instagram.com/colleenpaulhus4/
www.thePARC.com
www.sebringvideos.com

FROM NEVER TO FOREVER: EMBRACING A JOURNEY OF EDUCATION AND TRANSFORMATION

By Colleen Paul-Hus

In the pursuit of our purpose, the phrase "never say never" holds a profound significance.

It was during a casual visit to a local juice shop, engrossed in reading *Simplicity Parenting*, that a fertile seed was planted and my passion for education was awakened. A gentleman, noticing the book I held, recommended I read *Magical Child* by Joseph Chilton Pearce, revealing that his own childhood experiences in the Amazon rainforest mimicked the book's scientific findings. Intrigued, I knew I had to read it.

That book completely transformed my views on education and reinforced my intuitive belief in the boundless potential of humanity's hearts and minds.

Despite my having achieved what appeared to be the pinnacle of material success—a dream home near a prestigious private school, overlooking the ocean—my newfound understanding of human potential compelled me to seek alternative paths in education. Through *Magical Child*, Waldorf education and homeschooling emerged as viable options for our four young children. At that time, the local Waldorf school only extended to the third grade, so my husband and I chose to homeschool.

Yet, after two years, a desire for a like-minded community led us to revisit the local Waldorf school, now expanded up to the eighth grade. Soon after enrolling our children, I became deeply involved, serving as Co-Chairman of the school board and teaching Practical Arts and Gardening for six years. Although I poured my energy into nurturing the school's growth, I adamantly maintained that I would NEVER embark on opening my own educational institution.

Then came the year 2020—a year of unprecedented change and upheaval.

The pandemic forced families to homeschool, as well as prompted my family to seize the opportunity and invest time, resources, and energy into our 40-acre forest property in Sebring, Florida. Our endeavor at what later became the PARC began with building cabins, followed by a spacious open barn that would serve as the backdrop for homeschooling our children in nature's embrace. We developed a homeschool co-op centered around nature, academic studies, and practical skills. Word spread, and our homeschool co-op experienced surprising growth—from eight children in 2020 to fifteen in 2021, eventually reaching thirty in 2022. As demand continued to surge, we set our sights on attaining private school status and gave ourselves a name: The Academy at the PARC. Today, just three short years after opening, we have 80 enrolled children and are relentlessly working towards providing a unique educational experience and a model for educational innovation.

A typical day at our private school, The Academy at the PARC, begins with children tending to farm chores, from feeding the goats, chickens, ducks, and rabbits, to nurturing our garden and greenhouse. The children then head to their classrooms for a few hours of book work and academics. They take immense pride in their "cobin" classrooms, having actively participated in constructing them using earthen materials such as clay, straw, and sand. Following a morning of academic pursuits, the students break for lunch and recess before engaging in an afternoon of practical arts such as blacksmithing, woodworking, leatherworking, spoon carving, gardening, food harvesting, food preservation, and more. Practical arts is the hands-on application of knowledge acquired during the morning academic hours. Chemistry unfolds within the realm of blacksmithing, fractions manifest through cooking, geometry through leatherworking, and physics finds expression in the art of archery.

The brain discovers what the fingers explore.

Our focus is on using our bodies and hands to experience the WHY behind the academics. There are an enormous number of nerve endings in our fingertips; when we engage in hands-on activities and create with our hands, we stimulate these nerve endings, forging neural pathways in our brain that are integral to mathematical reasoning, language arts, creative expression, and gaining a deeper perspective on the world. As we train our hands to bring our ideas into tangible reality, an intricate dance unfolds between our hands and our heart. This dance, this synergy between the physical and the emotional, holds the key to unlocking heightened cognitive abilities in students.

The impact of this hands-on approach extends beyond the realm of skill acquisition. It nurtures holistic growth that encompasses not only the intellect but also the emotional wellbeing and character development of our students. Through the training of their hands, students cultivate resilience, patience, and a profound sense of accomplishment. They experience the joy of translating abstract concepts into concrete forms, and in so doing they realize their own capabilities and worth.

Reflecting on my journey, I couldn't help but trace back the roots of my passion for children and education. It stemmed from the struggles my brother faced within the traditional school system, where active kids were labeled with ADHD and medicated. Witnessing his challenges, his search for normalcy, and his eventual downward spiral, I knew something needed to change. I understood that the one-size-fits-all approach failed to accommodate the diverse needs and potential of each individual child. His schooling and childhood beyond 7 years old did not resemble the childhoods I read about in *Magical Child*. But it could have…

My journey has been one of transformation—guided by the profound understanding that purpose is not bound by the limitations we impose on ourselves. From declaring "never" to embracing a sense of purpose, I commit daily to create an environment that nurtures young minds and empowers them to believe in themselves and be valuable contributors to society. Today, my purpose lies in inspiring others to explore and create unique learning environments that integrate education, nature, nutrition, and emotional resiliency—an endeavor I once believed I would never undertake, but now wholeheartedly embrace.

My commitment to this work isn't fueled by financial gain; it's driven by the understanding that it's aligned with my purpose-driven calling.

I'm genuinely excited by the opportunity to share my story in a book that I intend to write. Navigating this journey that challenges established norms has presented me with a multitude of lessons. There were moments when I felt there was no way through the hurdles. Then, just as I approached the breaking points, subtle winks from God gave me the strength to persevere. What initially seemed like setbacks turned themselves into blessings in disguise. I now know that none of these challenges can rival the profound joy of witnessing the unwavering gleam in the eyes of the children—a light that doesn't fade, but instead has the potential to grow even brighter and more radiant.

Expert Tips:

Unveiling the Path to Purpose: How I Discovered Mine and How You Can Find Yours Too

1. Embrace the Escape: Amidst the upheaval of the 2020 pandemic, an unexpected escape unfolded. It was a journey that took me away from the hustle and bustle, leading me to the serenity of our property nestled in the woods. In this newfound solitude, I unearthed the gateway to my true

purpose. The escape doesn't have to be grand, but it is essential to create space where we can tune in to our inner voice. I detached myself from the relentless demands of daily life and allowed myself to truly connect. It was a connection with my higher self, a connection that thrived in harmony with the divine.

2. Reverence in Nature's Embrace: Surrounded by the unspoiled beauty of nature, I discovered a sanctuary where I could wholeheartedly connect to the source. Here, amidst the pristine authenticity of the natural world, I could hear the whispers that had eluded me before. Nature not only provided a space for me to cherish my family but also became the fertile ground where dreams took root. Our property, seen as a canvas awaiting our touch, beckoned us to tread humbly and work in harmony with God's creation. We vowed to preserve and nurture the precious trees that graced this sacred space, realizing that true creation lies in alignment with the gifts bestowed upon us.

3. Ignite the Vision: Vision flourishes when we unleash our playful nature, casting aside the limitations imposed by society. Dare to ask yourself, "What if?" and "Why not?" Let your imagination run wild as you dive into the depths of your vision. In vivid hues, paint the sights, sounds, and scents that form the tapestry of your dream. Imbue your vision with the fiery energy of emotion, for emotion is the very essence that breathes life into your dreams. Dance to the rhythm of your desires, and let music become the powerful amplifier of your aspirations. Energize your vision and infuse it with unstoppable determination.

4. Confronting Resistance: On the path to manifesting your vision, you will inevitably encounter resistance. It is through these challenges that you fortify yourself, readying your spirit

for the profound impact you are destined to make. Embrace these trials as stepping stones on your journey of growth and transformation. Do not succumb to despair or surrender to doubt. Remember, you are in the midst of training, honing the resilience necessary to touch countless lives through your creation. The greater the resistance, the more significant the impact your vision will have on others.

5. Listen and Adapt: Along your journey, listen attentively to the divine whispers, the gentle nudges that guide your steps. Stay attuned to the subtle signs and synchronicities, for they are the divine winks that illuminate your path. Adjust your vision as needed, remaining steadfast in your mission while embracing the fluidity of divine guidance. Adaptation allows your purpose to unfold in ways you may not have initially envisioned, yet it stays true to the core of your calling.

6. Service as the Guiding Light: Never forget that your gifts, your creation, your vision, are not for self-glorification but rather to serve others. Your purpose lies in illuminating the lives of those around you, in offering solace, inspiration, or transformation. By anchoring yourself in service, you forge a profound connection with humanity, extending the ripple effect of your purpose beyond measure.

As you embark on the journey of discovering your own purpose, remember that it is a voyage that is uniquely yours. Embrace the escape, forge a profound connection with nature, ignite your vision, confront resistance with unwavering determination, listen to the divine whispers, and let service be the compass that guides your path. May your journey be one of profound meaning and fulfillment as you align your existence with your true purpose.

Krystan Samaniego

MORE to Motherhood
Business Coach

Krystan Samaniego is the creator of a multi dimensional brand, MORE to Motherhood. She is a successful business coach, certified social media expert, and licensed financial educator. Krystan is happily married raising her three children in Florida.

Krystan became an entrepreneur in 2008 when she began working for herself as a Nationally Certified Sign Language interpreter across Florida.

Ultimately, she got into the Network Marketing space and after cracking the code to social media, she exploded her organization to 7-figures.

Krystan has been recognized as a top leader and top recruiter in the industry. She is an inspirational speaker and presenter on the topics of Social Media, Recruiting and Mindset. She has been a guest speaker on numerous podcasts, virtual events, and shared the stage with legends in the industry like Hal Elrod, Jessie Lee Ward, Kimberly Olson & Erin King just to name a few.

Krystan specializes in helping her clients with financial strategies, branding and social media marketing.

www.linkedin.com/in/krystan-samaniego
https://www.facebook.com/krystanasamaniego/
https://instagram.com/moretomotherhood
www.Moretomotherhood.com
https://msha.ke/moretomotherhood

OVERCOMING YOUR UPPER LIMITS

By Krystan Samaniego

Have you ever told yourself, "There has to be more to life than this." Or "I feel like I am meant to do something else, something more, with my life." If you have ever felt a calling in your heart for MORE, I am right there with you. I felt in my heart that I was meant for MORE for as long as I can remember, but I didn't act on it because I didn't know what that feeling was for the longest time.

People say the difference between the life you have and your dream life is ACTION. But I would also add MINDSET. The difference between the life you have and your dream life is ACTION & MINDSET.

I didn't actually act on my dreams or try to figure out what the calling in my heart was until I was sick and tired of being and feeling sick and tired.

I had overcome so much in my childhood, but as a young adult I found myself as a struggling single mom who had to move back in with her parents and new baby to start over. I had to declare bankruptcy. I was also on WIC and food stamps. I felt ashamed but I worked really hard to change my circumstances and was able to move out after a year and get a small apartment on my own for my son and I. I stepped up and was determined to give my son the life that a two parent household could provide. I was working a grueling sixty plus hours a week as a Nationally Certified Sign Language Interpreter. I had so much mom guilt and in hindsight I wish I spent more time with my son, instead of working so much to provide all of the things I thought he would want. I was burnt out and exhausted from constantly working outside of the home. I dabbled in Network Marketing as a hobby for a few years but never really saw it as a means to make a huge income, until I was sick and tired of being sick and tired.

I decided to approach my Network Marketing career as an actual business instead of a hobby. My husband and I had been married a few years by this point; we had two babies in daycare and my son needed therapy. We had great jobs, but I just didn't know how we could manage the girls in daycare and the cost of therapy that my son needed. I knew that I didn't want to make the same mistake twice working outside of the home and missing out on any more of my kids' childhood like I did with my son.

So, I decided to do something crazy. I hired a coach to teach me all about branding and marketing on social media. I was going to go back to Network Marketing and make six figures. I saw all these other women doing it and I thought, *Why can't I?*

I invested $10,000 that we didn't have on a credit card to pay for the coaching. My husband would have killed me if he found out (and I never did tell him, although I am sure he has heard me share the story by now).

I went all in! I DECIDED that my future was going to change and for the first time I believed I could do it; I had no other options.

A little over a month later I joined the Network Marketing company that would change my future. I did everything differently. I treated this side hustle like a business, not a hobby, and I walked into the bank after setting up my LLC and opened a business bank account. I remember sitting down with the banker and she asked me, "How much will your business make in a year?" I honestly had no idea; I had never really made enough money that it was worth opening an LLC and business account, but I told her that this business would make $100,000 in the first year. I felt so ridiculous saying it out loud, but I went with it. Literally a year later, almost to the day, my Network Marketing business made $100,000. I get chills every time I share that story because had I not put in the work to shift my mindset and my belief in myself, I would have never made a shift in my life. Once I discovered the true reason for building my business (my children), I became unstoppable in the pursuit of my goal, and I am here to tell you the same can happen for you! The journey is not always easy and like any entrepreneur there were a lot of highs and lows. I have definitely made a lot of mistakes in my career, but those mistakes have been lessons in my life that have taught me who I really am, what I am truly capable of and, ultimately, my passion in life.

Never give up on your goals and dreams, pursue that calling in your heart for MORE because you are made for MORE and we are Motivating Ourselves to Rise Everyday (M.O.R.E). As long as you continue to do that you will be unstoppable!

Here are my tips on how I overcame my upper limits and developed a Success Mindset.

Expert Tips: Developing a Success Mindset

We are all brought up with a preconceived notion of money, and our money story is developed throughout our childhood. This is obviously subconscious; but our subconscious is powerful.

As an entrepreneur we venture into the unknown, take risks, and at times it is hard to combat those negative thoughts and feelings of "what if?" Sometimes we don't even know we have them because they're deep in our subconscious.

- Hire a mindset coach

  I have found this to be the most important aspect of any business. We can have all the skills and tools to be successful, but if our brain is constantly battling us 24/7, subconsciously telling us we aren't worthy or money doesn't grow on trees (I know I heard that phrase often as a child) or that wealthy people are snobs or greedy… those impact our brain and how we operate. These thoughts are our upper limits. So, hiring a coach, someone to teach you how to eliminate and overcome these low vibrations, is a must. Anytime I have had major success in my business it's because I had a coach and I'm diligently working on my mindset daily. It's not easy to stay "high vibration" and positive all day, so someone to show you the way, continuously support you, and instill belief is essential.

- Develop a morning routine.

When I had the most success in business, I would take an hour throughout my morning to go through my morning routine. As a busy mom, I'm not saying sit down for an hour of uninterrupted time to go through your morning routine—we all know we can't even go to the bathroom alone without being interrupted—but break it up into small chunks throughout your morning or even throughout your day. I'll give you an example of what I did:

I recorded my affirmations, ideal day, and principles and goals very specifically, with details, smells, colors, and feelings where applicable. I listened to those recordings on my way to work or when I was driving in my car, and I would get chills and goosebumps of excitement (this is when you know it's working). Say it with feeling and excitement like you are speaking life into these affirmations and goals. I would write out my top ten goals every day as if I had already achieved them and five things I'm grateful for. I would also either do EFT tapping for five minutes or my meditation app—If I had extra time on the weekends I made sure to do this all throughout the day. Lastly, if you know me, I'm extra so I had a giant whiteboard of money goals and people I wanted to join me, and I even wrote and manifested/visualized goals for my team, too.

- Read books that enhance your habits and improve your mindset.

  My faves are Jack Canfield's *Success Principles* and Jenn Sincero's *You Are a BadAss at Making Money*

Lastly, brain dump every negative thought you have about money, success, yourself, or anything at all and then categorize and negate those beliefs with positive affirmations. Say them to yourself, write them every day or listen to a recording, but get those out of your head and visualize your success because you are worthy!

For more tips on mindset or coaching reach out! I would love to help you.

You are made for MORE!

Sarah Mathews Dean

BLONDIES LLC
Salon Professional

Sarah exudes passion in all she does! She is a proud mom of a beautiful daughter and an English Sheepdog, Charleigh!

With over 20 years' experience as a salon professional, Sarah is also the owner of Blondies LLC—a successful business she built by providing professional and trendy hairstyles and services to her clientele. Sarah loves working with her clients, inspiring them to be the best version of themselves inside and out.

Sarah has extensive experience in marketing, data analysis, sales, management skills and visual merchandising. Combining business experience and technique proved to be the perfect storm for her success in the beauty industry. Sarah also spent 15 years providing instruction to hairstylists across the United States as a Redken platform artist.

Sarah developed a unique passion for hiking and has climbed Mount Kilimanjaro five times. Her dedication, commitment and discipline inspires her clients every day.

https://www.facebook.com/sarah.dean.313
https://www.instagram.com/sarah_dean/

LESSONS ABOVE THE CLOUDS

By Sarah Mathews Dean

You may have heard the anonymous quote, "A good stylist is cheaper than a good therapist." Hair stylists often become very good listeners for their clients, but I believe we also can have a great influence. The "hair chair" is a unique place to share life journeys, experiences, interests, and different perspectives all while getting pampered. Over the years that I have had the honor and privilege to share my gifts and talents with clients, I have also recognized the opportunity I have to inspire, encourage, and enlighten them. I haven't taken this for granted, and my ability to connect with people through my work has truly become my purpose driven paycheck.

I'm Sarah Mathews Dean, a mom, Christian, hairdresser, endurance athlete, ice bath and plant-based diet lover and a hiker, living in Tulsa, Oklahoma. I grew up in a small town with a population of 1000; my dad is the town doctor there. Small town values I believe were the foundation of my character. Both of my parents instilled values that I subconsciously live everyday.

In this phase of my life my dad, George William Mathews (also known as Bill), is the inspiration for my Kilimanjaro journey—not to leave out my mom, because she is a badass also. Dad and I started running races together which soon led to hiking Pikes Peak in Colorado. We shared a love for a challenge and for being outside. In 2002 he climbed Mount Kilimanjaro with a doctor friend who shared his mind for adventure. I thought it was so cool but I was in "baby world"—my daughter was born in 2001 and there was no way for me to go or to afford such a trip, But it was definitely on my bucket list. In honor of our accomplishments we got matching tattoos—a sketch of the mountain, KMJ representing Kilimanjaro, and the year of our summits—on

Father's Day, his on his shoulder and mine on my wrist; agreeing on that was part of the excitement.

Since high school I knew I wanted to "do hair." I was the one doing prom hair and makeup in my bedroom. After high school and taking a gap year I went to college for three years, only to find out it wasn't my jam. Finally, in 2004, when my daughter was a year and a half, I took the plunge and went to Jenks Beauty School. Thankfully her father was supportive of this next move in my life. While in beauty school I knew I wanted more for my clients than just being behind the chair. I wanted more education and to bring my clients the most up to date styles, trends, and products. Soon I fell in love with Redken! They offered everything from principles to business and I knew I wanted to work for them. After many hours of continuing education, tests, and auditions, I became a Redken Platform Artist, and worked with them for 15 years, inspiring and teaching stylists all over the US while maintaining a successful business behind the chair.

The journey to Kili was still in the back of my mind—it just didn't seem possible. How could a person like me afford or even get to Africa, alone? On April 2nd, 2015, I was invited to a special training for educators in NYC. There they announced a leadership adventure for anyone in the room to hike Mount Kilimanjaro. And at that moment my journey had begun. 40 signed up and five went.

After a year of training, saving money, and collecting gear, I was ready to take on five nights and seven days on the mountain above the clouds. The night before my first climb at the hotel the clouds cleared and there she was: All six ecosystems and 19,341ft of her. She was ginormous and beautiful. *'No going back now,'* I thought. I was committed to getting to the summit.

Day one I was waiting at the gate to start up the mountain taking the Machame route (dad took the Marangu route) carrying a 15lb backpack, watching the porters work as a team carrying tents, food, tables and chairs, cooking supplies, and every climber's mountain duffel (on their heads) along with their own backpack. Their strength, willingness, and work ethic was admirable. They passed us on the mountain and the person in the back would shout "porter on the left!" so we all knew to move out of the way for them to pass. And by the time we got to camp every tent was set up ready for us. Sometimes they would be singing and dancing when we got to camp. Gratitude was overflowing. The first night sleeping in a tent on the ground takes some getting used to; the nights were very cold. The cooks would fill up our Nalgene water bottles with hot water and I would hold it like a baby to stay warm inside of the sleeping bag—I was so thankful for that. But the energy from the mountain filled me up. At night I did a lot of thinking about my daughter and my relationships and tried to find a way to forgive myself for all the mistakes I made. I usually cried myself to sleep leaving guilt behind. Each day on the mountain presented different landscapes (and, of course, altitude); I was falling in love with Kili. The little voice in my head would say "Are we ever going to get to the summit?" At times all I could think about was getting that picture by the sign and posting so my clients and family could see my accomplishment. Every step felt like I was adding a penny to the jar and trying to get to a million dollars. Step...rest...pressure breath...was the name of the game. The pressure breath helps you to get more oxygen back in—along with drinking a gallon of water and electrolytes and eating a lot of food. Daily we would check our blood oxygen levels to ensure we were climatizing. On day four if your oxygen levels are low and your body won't acclimate you are forced to leave the mountain. I watched this happen twice with family members making hard choices—*do I go on without you?*

Both were fathers saying goodbye to their children and wife. Tears, hugs, and prayers as they each went their separate ways. The lesson—

love! I created a mantra that I still use to this day when I'm hiking: "I am healthy (step) I am strong (step) I love this mountain (step) thank you God (step)," forcing myself to be present, look around, and take in God's creation. It's easy to look down and just get to the top. I finally learned this lesson on my third trek up Kili. Seven days on the mountain and people can start to get on your nerves; altitude can intensify that feeling along with dealing with your own bullshit. But looking back the things that drove me crazy were the things I dislike about myself or faults I saw in myself. Summit day, we wake at 3am and start climbing. At 5am it's so dark and cold, fingers and toes are numb, and it's definitely mental because the sun will rise and bring warmth. I stopped and turned toward the sun appearing over the curve of the horizon. I could feel the earth move; God was there, it doesn't get any closer to him than that. We made it to Uruhu peak. On my second time up Kili I almost didn't make it to Uruhu. My oxygen levels were low because I didn't properly prepare; I took for granted how easy it was for me the first time. After taking medicine my numbers went up and I summitted, but I didn't feel good about it. My third time on Kili I was coming back for redemption. Taking the lessons from the first two treks up Kili I reached Uruhu for the third time. But God wasn't done with me, we still had some work to do. After three trips on Kili I had to show others how to have this adventure and experience. I wanted my own team. So I started by sharing and encouraging my clients to commit to life a changing experience. On trips four and five I took my hair chair clients. Preparing them from start to finish and watching them on the journey was so cool. Being their team leader forced me to be diligent with my own training, and I loved that!

People ask me "why five times?" Until I wrote this chapter I couldn't answer that question. I was called back, I had more learning and healing to do. Life above the clouds with no distractions looks so different, but it doesn't always feel good. Letting go of all the crap that takes up space in your heart is painful, but the reward is realizing you're a badass. Being comfortable and safe is dangerous. You don't have to climb mountains but you have to do hard things to grow. The scarier the better! Educate yourself and walk the walk. Keep reaching for the summit of your mountain.

Expert Tips: Trust the process

Trust—belief, truth, strength.

Process—series of actions to achieve a goal.

I watched "trust the process" unfold before my eyes. My daughter was training for a bodybuilding competition. Everyday she would prep and weigh out her food and eat it at certain times. Each day she would train a different body part to achieve overall symmetry and fuel her body after with shakes and supplements. Doing cardio in the morning before food. Everything she did had a process and was done with intention. Every day was hard but that didn't phase her; she had her eye on the prize. I watched as her discipline, mental strength, consistency, love, and celebrations transformed her body. And she shined on stage and won her competition.

- Love your goal
  Love your goal and it will love you back.
  Be starving for it.
  Do it scared—love cancels out fear.
  Never take it for granted.

- Be present on the journey
  Even when it hurts—stay in the pain.
  Don't think about when this training session will be over, or how much longer you have.
  Stop, enjoy, and look around.

- Celebrate all wins
  Small steps lead to big steps, as I learned on Kili.
  Be proud of all of your accomplishments.
  Choose happiness.
  Even if you messed up—you learned!

- Mental Preparation
  When you think you're dying you're actually living.
  Breathe—I prefer the Wim Hof method.
  Visualize yourself reaching your summit.
  Make hard changes

- Consistency/Discipline
  When faced with a choice, make the hard, RIGHT one—the easy choice is usually the wrong one.
  Show up and follow the plan even when you don't feel like it.
  Uncomfortable is the new normal.
  Get an accountability partner when you're struggling to get it done.
  Don't cheat yourself—you're only filling a void.
  Plan.

Jessika Fielder

Always Virtual Solutions
Virtual Assistant

Jessika Fielder is a former teacher and now current virtual assistant and social media manager. She has been doing this for three years and absolutely loves it! Jessika has always loved helping people, which is why she became a virtual assistant and social media manager. She has worked with a variety of coaches, small businesses and entrepreneurs. She is happily married and living in Northern Nevada, but she was born and raised in San Diego, California. She has her Masters in Education and a California and Nevada teaching credential. When Jessika is not helping her clients, she loves to travel with her husband and fur-baby, Baxter.

https://www.linkedin.com/in/jessika-fielder-4701517a/
https://www.facebook.com/jessika.fielder.1
https://www.instagram.com/j_fielder2/
https://alwaysvirtualsolutions.com/home/

HOW TO BECOME A SUCCESSFUL VIRTUAL ASSISTANT

By Jessika Fielder

Have you ever thought about working virtually or being your own boss? Does the thought of helping run someone else's business sound appealing to you? Have you ever heard of a virtual assistant or social media manager? I have been doing both of these jobs for three years and absolutely love it! As a former teacher, I have learned how to be flexible and organized while managing multiple tasks, which are important characteristics of a virtual assistant.

I became a virtual assistant and social media manager three years ago because I wanted the flexibility to work where I want, when I want. I absolutely love helping people and helping others succeed, which I am able to do as a virtual assistant. I am able to help businesses grow and become more successful by offering my services. In the past, I have had various jobs that include customer service, administration, advising, and teaching, which have all been beneficial to my role as a virtual assistant.

A virtual assistant is someone (typically a freelancer or someone who is self-employed) who works virtually (outside an office), helping businesses or entrepreneurs with various tasks on a daily and/or weekly basis. Some of these tasks could include customer service, calendar management, email inbox management, project management, event planning, web development, copywriting, social media, transcription, translation, and data entry.

So, why would someone hire a virtual assistant? Virtual assistants have become very popular over the past few years. During the pandemic, many business owners and entrepreneurs realized that they needed help with various tasks, since they were working from home. In other cases, they simply do not want to nor have the time to complete the tasks that a virtual assistant could complete for them. This is where someone like me comes in! If someone is exhausted from working all the time, struggling with work/life balance, wanting to focus on other tasks or just needs help, I step in to take tasks off their plate.

Another appealing reason to hire a virtual assistant is the financial benefits. In most cases, you are a freelancer or an independent contractor, so your client does not have to worry about paying your taxes, paying for any sort of insurance or providing equipment, an office, or supplies. As an independent contractor, you are responsible for all of that, which can be very appealing to your clients.

It is actually quite simple to become a virtual assistant. Although there are courses you can take and coaches you can hire, essentially you just need to figure out what you are good at and enjoy doing. Ask yourself, "what are my strengths and what do I truly enjoy?" From there, you can either apply to jobs with those tasks or advertise your services. Also, if you can narrow down your services to something that is unique or in high demand, you will have better luck getting jobs. This is referred to as "niching down," since you will attract a certain person who needs your help. But don't worry—you can always change your ideal client as you become more accustomed to being a virtual assistant. Furthermore, even reaching out to your network for opportunities or referrals could get you clients or jobs. Knowing who you want to work with will help you avoid issues in the future and make your business more successful. You will feel more valued and useful if you are working with someone that you love to help.

One of the first things to do when becoming a virtual assistant is to determine your rate of pay. In many situations, virtual assistants charge either by the hour or a monthly package rate. When determining your rate or package prices, the best way is to decide how much you want to make each month and then divide that by how many hours you want to work each week. For example, if you want to make at least $1,000 a month and only want to work 40 hours a month, your starting rate would be $25 an hour. In some situations, I will adjust my charge based on the complexity of the task(s). If the potential client proposes a different rate than you prefer, this is where you have the luxury to decide whether or not to work with them. Again, knowing your financial "deal breakers" will be very helpful in finding your ideal client. Just keep in mind that you need to make enough to cover your own taxes, insurance, etc.

One of the biggest misunderstandings in becoming a virtual assistant is that you need to have everything set up and completed (website, landing page, email list, training, etc.) before starting work or advertising your services. This is definitely not true! My best advice is to just get started. You do not have to wait until everything is ready to go. If you know that you want to be a virtual assistant, do not wait! All that you really need is a way to meet potential clients (such as social media), a contract, and a way to take payments and you are good to go! All of the rest can come as you go. You can always read blogs and other resources to continue to expand your knowledge, which is what I do. I am constantly reading articles so that I can improve and become more advanced. This also helps you to continue to always be knowledgeable about new trends and techniques so that you do not become "stuck in your ways."

The joy of being a virtual assistant is that you can work from anywhere and choose who you work with (at least within a certain specialty, such as a coach, mentor, speaker, etc.). You have the freedom to work wherever you want, whether you are working at home in your pajamas, in a coffee house, a library, or anywhere else. You also have the pleasure of choosing the tasks that you perform and offering those tasks to specific potential clients. In many cases, you can even choose how many hours you work per week. When speaking to a potential client, you can mention how many hours you want to work each week, and whether you want only one client or multiple clients. Plus, a lot of your tasks can be completed from your phone!

So, you may be thinking, "What skills or traits do I need to have in order to be a virtual assistant?" Since you will be working virtually, many clients are unable to "check-in" with you like they would be able to if you were in an office. In many situations, entrepreneurs and business owners are looking for people who are reliable, organized, good communicators, hard working, efficient, and good at managing their time. All of these skills will help you to create a positive and long-lasting relationship with your client. In many situations, I will either send a client a daily or weekly recap of what I completed, so that they know that I am completing my tasks. With past clients, I have even had a quick check-in at the beginning and/or end of the week to go over everything that was completed and what still needs to be done. This helps reassure the client that I am dependable and that both of us are staying on track.

So, after all this, you may be wondering how you find your ideal client. The main thing is networking and marketing. I mainly use social media to create relationships with people that I would want to work with. I have also joined various Facebook groups to either connect with people looking for a virtual assistant or to advertise my services. You can also use other platforms, such as Instagram, LinkedIn, etc. to market yourself. The key is to stay consistent with posting your services so that people know what you do and where to find you. The more consistent you are, the more people will see you and the better the chance that you will find your ideal client. When promoting yourself, try to come up with an "elevator pitch." This is typically a one sentence phrase that describes who your ideal client is and what you can do for them. This could be something as simple as "I help (describe your ideal client) by (say what you can do for them)." Make sure to make your elevator pitch very clear and short. This will help people know exactly how you can help them!

Being a virtual assistant has completely changed my life and I love what I do! I love working with people that I know I can help. It may seem scary to start this journey at the beginning, but I am sure that you will love it as much as I do! Just remember: if this is something that you want to do, don't quit!

Expert Tips:

- **Niche down/specialize:** Focusing on a specific task or profession will help you find your ideal client who you will love working for. Focus on your strengths, not duties that you will be completing. When focusing on your strengths, you will be using a lot of your skills and talents, which will help you support your client on a deeper level.

- **Set pricing that will benefit you:** Remember that you will have to pay for your own taxes, insurance, and supplies so make sure that you are factoring those aspects into your hourly or package rates. Do not be afraid to tell your future client your rate or reduce the rate because you need the money. Your ideal client will gladly pay for you and your services!

- **Build confidence by always learning:** Continuing to stay up to date on resources, tips, and tasks will help you diversify your skill set and be more appealing to clients. This also shows your client that you are assertive and willing to adjust to something new and continue to learn.

- **Network/advertise:** Always network with potential clients and advertise your services. If someone doesn't know what you do, they will not be able to hire you. Join groups that would have your ideal client in them. Remember to always use your elevator pitch.

- **Set clear expectations:** This is something that you want to do from the beginning. Make sure that both you and the client know the expected work hours, hourly rate, and days. This will prevent burn-out and create a positive relationship between the two of you. If there are certain days or times that you cannot or do not want to work, make sure to express these in the beginning. Communication is key!

- **Know your value and worth:** Your client needs you, which is why they hired you, so know that you are important and should not be taken advantage of. This is also where setting clear expectations in the beginning is important.

- **Create a website or landing page (eventually):** Although this does not have to be done before you start advertising your services, it is a good idea to have one so that potential clients can see all of your services. In the beginning, you can even just create a one page resume that lists your services and qualifications to send to prospective clients. This will help ensure that you are attracting your ideal clients and completing tasks that you feel are your strengths.

- **Don't quit:** It can be discouraging when you do not get any clients, but do not quit! Keep advertising and networking. Be consistent. Continue learning. Use your elevator pitch and your ideal client will come around!

Stacey Duncan

Duncan Group
Entrepreneur

Stacey Duncan is a nationally accomplished lending originator. She has been in the top 2% of her industry's production by volume for a decade and top 1% of women's originators throughout the country. By the age of 30, she successfully sold two lending practices; partnered with a large national lender and created 17 joint ventures. Teaching them to build wealth thru monetizing single transactions.

Her life has not been conducive for the lifestyle she lives today. She is humbled knowing that her success comes from the foundation of consistency and willpower.

"If you believe you can, you will."

Stacey was off and on homeless until the age of 7, and then lived with multiple family members throughout her childhood years. As a cancer survivor she sees time with intention as her biggest asset; focusing on showing her two girls that they can take over the world and raise a family.

https://www.linkedin.com/in/staceyduncan/
https://www.facebook.com/acleanclose
https://www.instagram.com/mortgagemindsetcoach/
www.carolinalending.com

INCHING TOWARD YOUR QUANTUM LEAP

By Stacey Duncan

I was born into a household in California where drugs were used as frequently as most people would have a daily cup of coffee. My father was ten years older than my mother, and their explosive relationship ultimately led to my relocation to the Carolinas, where I currently reside. I knew no fairy tales, Santa, or Easter Bunny from an early age. Life was raw, honest, and very messy. Until the age of seven, we were homeless, sleeping in the back of our green, very rusted Oldsmobile Cutlass Supreme. I remember counting the reflectors on the side of the road as we drove and spending days in the hot California sun playing in the park because we had nowhere else to go. Food was scarce, and exposure to the harsh realities of life shaped my outlook on resilience and determination, which became the foundation of my success.

When I was seven, my grandmother gained custody of me and relocated me to the Carolinas, where she raised me until she passed away when I was thirteen. From then on, my housing was unstable, and I stayed with multiple family members throughout the years until I moved out early and put myself through school. I started working a summer job in mortgages and somehow survived. Without a mentor or a healthy work environment, I did what any logical, naive twenty-year-old would do: I didn't give up. I was the first person in the office each day and the last to leave every day. Within a year, I made $40,000 a month in commissions, outproducing people fifteen years my senior. I smiled, stayed focused, and had a lot of jealous people in my office who would comment on my success. Remember, this was an income-earned commission. There was no way to trick the system but to work and show up, even on sick days.

At 23, I walked out and knew I wanted a better culture for my business.

I quit my job and opened a lending institution franchise called a Net Branch. If I were going to hit a wall or fail, it would be on my terms. I worked a lot. I woke up, went to work, went home, went to bed, and repeated. Everything I did, thought, ate, read, and watched was related to this career. I lived under a rock, and as some of my team members now tell me, I still do. At that age, I felt invincible. I was in the phase of life where I knew it all, and no one with wisdom could tell me otherwise until I got cancer the first time.

Not to be religious, but I think it took God to humble me in a place where I would not allow any human to enter. Being openly vulnerable has never been my strong suit. For the first time as an adult, I was out of control. Shattered. I wanted to cry, be angry. My ego wasn't ready for the treatments, surgeries, side effects, and thoughts of not being enough. I was a victim sitting inside a warrior's body, taking up headspace, telling myself that I should quit or give up on my dreams. I didn't know how to love myself during a time when that was all I needed.

I don't know how to explain it, but I woke up one morning, and a light switch in me flipped from angry and helpless to determined and focused. This time, there was no ego leading the way to destroy my future self, no opportunity I had missed that wasn't meant for me, and no pity party. I loved myself and wanted to show myself I was worth fighting for when all seemed hopeless. Not even a year later, I started another company, a commercial brokerage, that I sold during a steep downturn of the real estate market. We did this by building opportunity and intention for what the appetite of our investors needed weekly—managing syndicate funding, hedge investments, and staying consistent with our actions daily while others played chess trying to outrun their reality and regroup with fear rather than focus.

Don't get me wrong; I saw some people who have worked harder than most lose everything they had during this time, which was terrible. I am not saying we beat the system just because of what we did. We took advantage of more one-on-one time, hit the streets and made new contacts when people stuck to what they felt comfortable with and didn't cut their losses early, ending with them losing their life savings. These were my character-building years. The times when you want to give up, but you somehow keep dragging yourself day in and day out to inch closer to your goals. It's impossible to give up when your purpose and your passion are more significant than your path to get there.

Fast forward 20 years later, and building up to today, I have survived cancer multiple times. So much so that I treat it like a tune-up, conducting a gut check, heart check, and mindset shift assessment annually, regrouping my sphere. Throughout this timeline, I have been among the top 1% of women producers in the country in our industry, attending company and client meetings between doctor's appointments and scheduling surgeries around long holiday weekends. Cancer has motivated me to maintain three foundational focuses: consistency, resilience, and perseverance. Luckily, we have grown, even in this economic downturn due to COVID, where 40% of our industry is no longer viable. This is all because we have remained in a space where most give up right before they reach it, that 1% space where grit and glory meet moments before you think you are about to hit a wall, and you take a leap of faith and keep pushing.

To attain growth, you need to limit your sphere. I used to open my life raft for everyone until I realized that when people see you succeeding while they are drowning, they will poke a hole in the float you're sharing to drown you both. It is human nature for most. Limiting your sphere to people who believe in themselves and clap for you when you are not in the room is who you need to surround yourself with, not the ones who will defend why they were not clapping. You cannot grow with weeds; it takes resilience to break your heart a few times to find your tribe.

Self-employment or tackling any significant move to grow in your career will come with its fair share of hurdles. Some of them will hit you so hard that it knocks the wind out of you, and you will have days when you feel like you are gasping to breathe. Take a moment for yourself to ground your emotions. Walking, calling a friend, or something as simple as playing your favorite song can help you refocus your mindset and make a checklist of why you are fighting so hard to achieve your goal. Remember, walking purposefully and recounting your "why" will be the key to perseverance. You made it this far, which means life is ever-changing—the evolution of a diamond is not pretty.

A few years ago, I lost my dad to cancer, and he passed away on Thanksgiving, ironically my favorite holiday. Shortly after, I went through a tough time in my marriage, which I do not talk about often. During that time, I learned that you need to refocus to overcome. Revisit your purpose and passion when things seem the hardest. All the little things in those moments no longer cloud your vision. Take the time for yourself on your worst days, reflect on the importance of where you want to be, and let it teach you repeatedly how to love and be loved. Self-care and self-awareness will take you in your business and life to places you did not know were possible. When we forget to regroup around our passion and purpose, we get sidetracked and derail our vision.

Your consistent efforts will gain more traction than the most intelligent man in the room every single time. There is no competition when you are the only one there. Your resilience to take a hit by the industry, market, company you keep, or life in general will set you apart from the 99% of your competition that uses these hurdles as an excuse to quit. Your persistence when you have been rejected the first or one-thousandth time will make or break the level of success you attain. If you take the word no as your answer, you are asking the wrong person or phrasing the question in a way that doesn't meet their needs. The last mile, the home stretch, the right before you achieve greatness or make a move to alter the trajectory of your life, is a time that needs to be fueled by passion and purpose and nothing less.

Expert Tips:

- Write your goals down freehand and revisit what you want to accomplish in three months, six months, one year, five years, ten, and twenty.

- In terms of business, personal, health, financial, spiritual, romance, recreational (in no particular order), where do you want to be in these milestone years of your life?

- Look at these weekly and if any of them do not resonate as deeply as the others, mark through them. The remaining ones are how you are to build the trajectory of your vision and things that take away from that you are to ignore or remove yourself from them.

- Start limiting your sphere. That doesn't mean you ditch Aunt Linda, who doesn't understand your dream of being a Youtuber. It means you categorize whose words you take to heart and who in your circle are your tribe. You cannot succeed without the support, and being angry at people who do not believe in themselves, let alone someone else, will cloud your vision.

- There is no crying in _____. You can insert your career here. Your emotions are a reaction to things broken in your business. Sometimes you must fix your vision to fix your mission and know that facts are the foundation of your future. It is hard to swallow when you must self-reflect and raise your hand to admit that you are the problem.

- Remember, no one climbed Mount Everest alone; they had a

camera crew if they did. Gratitude is the key ingredient to gaining support from peers and affiliates in your field, and humility attracts that success repeatedly.

- Did you thank the janitor? A silly sentence, but the things you take for granted as you build your empire are vital ingredients and staples to your success. Sometimes, you are the janitor. Cleaning up your business will be a constant labor of love. No title or role is too small as you gain momentum financially; remember, being kind and showing compassion is always free.

- Train past the finish line. Most in professional sports or the Olympics train as hard as they can to get to the finish line and those who go home with the gold train ten steps further. Remember, you must account for the weather in a race or any event. Turbulence, problems, and hurdles, and the one thing holding you back to greatness, was that you set your goals to a place where you could achieve them without loss. The larger the goal you didn't reach, the greater the reward of where you'll make it.

- Remember that success comes in different stages of our lives. You are swimming, trying to beat your best time. Stay in your lane and focus on your craft for long-term success. Wanting to win so that you can beat Cousin Larry at the county fair's hot dog eating contest isn't enough to stay successful. It would be best if you had a purpose for your vision.

- Revisit how to stay in a position to thrive often. Gaining your throne and being complacent leaves room for someone else to take it.

Debbie Worthington

CEO of Briwen Faith LLC

Debbie Worthington is an Insurance Professional and a Real Estate Investor. She is a single mother of two and raising her children has been her greatest blessing in her life. Debbie has overcome much adversity in her life and attributes that to her faith in God and her mindset.

Debbie is an award winning sales person and started her first business in the wireless industry as a dealer for multiple cellular carriers. When she realized that the wireless industry was changing and she knew she needed a back up plan, she started an Insurance Agency to create more residual income.

Debbie is passionate about helping others get their house in order (wills, life insurance, retirement). As a Real Estate Investor she specializes in helping distressed homeowners as well as runs communities of people learning Real Estate Investing. Debbie has won multiple awards in Sales, Leadership and Building Teams. She is passionate about helping people achieve their best life.

https://www.linkedin.com/in/debbie-worthington-92537224/
https://www.facebook.com/debbie.b.worthington
https://www.instagram.com/debbie.b.worthy/
https://web.zybrzeus.com/debbie/debbie/

DON'T SETTLE EVER!

By Debbie Worthington

Are you worthy of success? Do you care too much about what others think? Are you happy and fulfilled? What does all of that even mean? Most of us do all the things we are supposed to do, right?! I mean, we go to college and/or get jobs, pay bills, raise kids, pay taxes, and follow the rules of society. We have been programmed this way and if we are lucky, we get to take a week of vacation each year. Right??!!! Nooooo!!

The older I get the more I feel like we were created to live much bigger lives! God wants us to live BIG! Think about it, the human body and mind can do so many amazing, miraculous things and most of us do not achieve all that we are capable of!

Most of my life I have been too worried about what others think about me and about what they think I'm supposed to be doing. I didn't feel worthy of success. As I learned about mindset and the subconscious mind, I started on a mission to reprogram my thinking and get out of my own way. My name is Debbie Worthington and I grew up in Atlanta, GA, and I have settled for most of my life. My message to myself and to anyone else who wants to listen is Please Do Not Settle! Life is too short and you are the only one who will fight for you. Don't miss out!

Fortunately, I was a terrible W2 employee. I always knew I wanted more, but I wasn't sure how to get it. My first business was a wireless business—a cellular dealer. At the time I was working for a wireless carrier in sales and wanted to start my own company. I cashed out my stock which came to $26,000 and bought my first cell phone inventory. My children were little, and I remember being in my very first store and looking around and feeling such a moment of satisfaction and joy, because I had actually pulled it off. Working in the wireless business, I had some fabulous months of revenue. I also ended up getting divorced during this time, so I became a single mom. As the industry started changing along with the commissions, I worried about having to raise my children on my own, and started to figure out what I could do to add to that revenue. As a single mom, I knew I was going to have to come up with a plan; I got into insurance and became appointed with many insurance carriers. I imagined residual income and helping people—the funny thing about insurance is you have to have money in order to start; all I had at this point was my wireless business. I used that business as my cash flow to start this new endeavor. Before I could even get my new business going, the real estate crash began in 2007 and lingered throughout 2009. The aftermath of the crash went on for a while— most of my clients in the wireless business were builders, builder supply houses, real estate brokerages and so on. Most of them shut down and business went away. Things began to get very scary and financially difficult. And here I was with three high dollar beautiful retail store fronts, two businesses, two kids, and employees who had families to feed too. I even started to pay these employees out of my own personal credit lines. I did not pull the trigger fast enough as everything was crashing down around me. I moved both businesses into one location and eventually moved them into my house and let the employees go. At that point, I was riddled with debt and scared to death! The thing that helped me to climb out of that was sheer determination and visualization of what I really wanted. I'll never forget the day I had only $300 in my bank account and I had to send my children off with my mom and sister to go on a vacation. My kids and I had always gone on fun trips together but I just did not have the money this time. I was drowning—or really I had already drowned. I remember just sitting and wondering what I was going to do. Here I was in a spare bedroom in my house with two businesses and no employees. I started willing myself to get through this and not let my kids down! I made my first vision board that day—I had always wanted to make one but never had. I also knew that if I did not change my mindset, this was not going to end well. That day in tears I started to crawl out of the hole. My wireless business received a phone call from a client in the trucking business that I had almost forgotten I had. They had plans for big growth and I was able to help them come up with a plan for apps on their phones to help their drivers work more safely and efficiently. I turned my home into an assembly line of programming phones, shipping them out and packing up cell phone accessories with my children helping me. Everything on my vision board came true!

Throughout all of this I learned that I must have the determination and the desire to change and make a difference. I learned to believe strongly that I could overcome any obstacle thrown my way. And I also learned that visualizing it happening as if it had already happened was key as well. Without an all-consuming belief and desire it is hard to push yourself to achieve the results that you are looking for. You need to have a desire for something new, something that could change your life and causes you to reach deep within yourself for abilities you didn't know you had as well as reach for resources that you may have overlooked before.

It took me many years to really believe in myself and to push for my success. I knew I had to consistently fill my mind and environment with personal development and people who had already achieved what I was trying to do. I would like to encourage everyone to distance themselves from negativity. Figure out who you really are and what you really want. I so wish I would have done this years ago. The sky's the limit and most of the time we are our biggest obstacle. And this is true in your business and personal relationships as well! Don't make a decision based on what someone else will think. Don't quit. And definitely don't settle ever!

One of the best things that ever happened to me in my entrepreneurial career was finding a fabulous real estate investing community. It is much more than real estate investing—it is financial literacy, business ownership, personal development, and amazing relationships. There were so many things I did not know before I found this community in late 2015. I really had zero financial literacy skills and a scarcity mindset around money (and a lot of other things, actually). I went next-level with this business— I have done 31 real estate transactions; I have helped distressed homeowners; purchased properties at deep discounts; purchased tax liens and purchased properties creatively with very little money. We create cash flow-based retirement with rental properties and we pay less in taxes. I have decided that I'm never going to grow old because there will always be something new to learn. The cool thing is that I have a team that I've been building and I get to watch them do the same thing. I have people on my team of all ages building their rental portfolios;it's pretty incredible. And I have been able to create multiple revenue streams with this real estate investing community: one is in what we call the Wealth Cycle and the other is in my real estate transactions. If anyone has any interest in learning how to do real estate investing anywhere in the country, reach out to me at Debbie@worthingtonagency and I will be happy to assist. In this community there is room for all of us to succeed!

I am also passionate about people protecting their lives and taking care of their families. We always think we have more time, but we do not! I offer life insurance, health insurance, wills, retirement plans, and all sorts of life insurance including term, whole life, IULs, mortgage protection and more. I have a fabulous team of people and all major carriers that really understand these products, and we do reviews to make sure that we are meeting your needs and protecting you and your family. Please do not let your family go unprotected. Contact me here for a painless way to get some of these things handled for yourself and your family! https://web.zybrzeus.com/debbie/go/

Whatever you do, believe in yourself and push to create a life you love! You deserve it and no one will do it for you. Reach deep within to tap into your mental, physical and emotional power. Visualize everything you want to aid you in your belief. I believe in you!

Expert Tips: Belief Using Visualization

1. Decide what you want and who you want to be. Give this some serious thought. Dig deep. Do not fluff over this. You may reevaluate this as things shift in your life, but knowing this clearly helps your subconscious mind take steps and make decisions to lead you towards your desires.

2. Celebrate your wins and every step forward. This can boost your confidence and reinforce your belief in your abilities.

3. Reflect on your past successes. Remind yourself of the obstacles you have overcome and the goals you have already accomplished. Recognizing your past accomplishments can reinforce the belief that you have the capability to succeed.

4. Surround yourself with positivity and supportive people who believe in you. Seek out mentors, friends and family who inspire and encourage you. Their support can reinforce your self-belief and provide valuable guidance along your journey.

5. Practice positive self-talk. Monitor your inner dialogue and replace self-doubt and negative thoughts with positive affirmations. Repeat positive statements about your capabilities and visualize yourself succeeding in your desired outcomes.

6. Embrace failures as learning opportunities. Instead of viewing failures as setbacks, reframe them as opportunities for growth and learning. Learn from the failures for the next time but understand that setbacks are part of the journey and can help maintain belief in yourself and your abilities.

7. Consistently take action towards your goals. Taking regular and consistent action helps build momentum and instills confidence and belief in your ability to achieve.

8. Continuously learn and improve. Invest in your personal and professional development. Acquire new skills and seek knowledge. Expanding your knowledge and honing your skills will increase your competence and confidence in pursuing your dreams.

9. Visualize success. Make a vision board and change it out as you achieve the things you put on it—and you will achieve them.

Remember that building self-belief takes time and effort. Be patient with yourself and embrace the journey, as self-belief is a powerful force that can propel you towards your goals and aspirations.

Mike Gostola & Carla Shaw

Founder and CEO of RockTheTok Academy and Rise Marketing

Mike Gostola and Carla Shaw are entrepreneurs and online marketing strategists. With over a decade of experience, they've helped thousands of entrepreneurs ignite and scale their home businesses by leveraging Social Media, their own unique message, and Attraction Marketing.

Driven by a desire to uplevel the social selling industry, Mike and Carla share the techniques and strategies they have utilized to build their business to the top 1% of their company. Recognized by their ability to discover big ideas that transform the industry they have become expert trainers for Attractionmarketing.com and have trained thousands on how to leverage the power of TikTok with their industry-leading course RockTheTok.

Based in Calgary, Canada, Mike and Carla are proud parents of two adventurous children, a dog, a horse, and many reptiles. They believe that we are all capable of extraordinary achievements, and the world needs your unique message.

www.mikeandcarla.ca
https://www.facebook.com/groups/tiktokfornetworkmarketers
https://www.tiktok.com/@mike.gostola

THE POWER OF TWO: HOW TO BUILD A LEGACY BUSINESS WITH YOUR SPOUSE

By Mike Gostola & Carla Shaw

"You work with your spouse?" is a comment we both get often.

At first, it wasn't like that. We had both set out on our own path, for our own careers—Carla in marketing, and me in construction.

From day one we were both each other's biggest cheerleaders, supporting and encouraging each other to excel in our given fields.

We openly discussed our days and what they looked like, and we consulted with each other to determine the best path forward for whatever challenge we may be facing.

Before we were in business together, we were already in business together, we just didn't label it.

We were both very driven and focused on building a strong foundation in our chosen fields. We had set goals and had a path to follow to achieve these goals, but like most things in life, the universe had other plans for us...

Through a series of events, starting with me gaining weight, we stumbled into the world of online marketing.

At first, we resisted because all I really wanted was some products to improve my health, but soon we found ourselves in multiple conversations about what I was doing; we were earning awards and getting paid a pretty good income from sharing something that was working.

That was when both of our entrepreneurial minds kicked in. I had been building small businesses since I left high school, and Carla came from a family of entrepreneurs who had built multiple businesses. So naturally, we both were attracted to this new form of income.

At the time, we didn't have a concrete plan, we didn't have goals (gasp) and we had no clue how to really 'work' with each other. We just knew it felt right and it gave us a new, powerful vehicle to achieve our dreams.

However, something unexpected happened once we decided to treat it as a bona fide business, rather than a mere hobby—it became challenging for us to collaborate effectively, and it began to strain our marriage.

Pretty sure you know this—in marriage, emotions can run deep, especially when money and love are involved. But add in a business and you toss in another layer of complexity.

Here's the juicy truth, my friend: it doesn't have to be a wild, crazy rollercoaster of emotions and it does not have to be hard.

What if I whispered a little secret in your ear?

There's a magical alchemy that can turn those intense emotions into rocket fuel that propels your partnership and allows you to jump ahead in your business.

Because when you can figure out how to leverage each other's strengths, tap into those emotions, and be focused on goals that benefit your family as a whole, absolute magic can happen.

What we discovered along the way was that we both had aspects of our business that lit us up and we both had aspects of our business that sucked the energy from us.

It was at that point that we found the magic sauce, the glue to stick it all together.

By identifying our strengths and passions, we were able to jump timelines in our business.

Things that used to drag us down and stall our growth were delegated out and we leveraged our strengths and were open about where we didn't thrive.

And that 'emotion' that was getting in the way before? We learned how to tap into it. We realized that emotion, when used in the right way, is an incredible fuel. With open communication, honesty, and grace we were able to channel it and use it to our advantage.

We hope that if you're reading this now, you'll skip over years of struggle and have a clear plan for how to ignite your business as a couple and a family.

How did we uncover all this?

It started with a trip to Las Vegas.

It was our first time going to a business growth event together. At that event we realized that we couldn't get the results we wanted from the actions we were taking; our partnership was working in life, but not in business.

We had to pivot.

So we DID. We dove head first into training and mentorship, stepping out of our comfort zones both together and on our own.

We invested heavily in ourselves, we got vulnerable with each other and with our mentors, and we committed to building a business that would give us the time and financial freedom we were looking to give to our children.

It felt like we were on the right path. There was still sooo much we didn't know and so many hard lessons to learn.

Like any business, it is important to put the right people in the right seats on the bus, but when doing it as a couple, with only two people in the business, who ARE MARRIED, who gets to drive...?

You both do!

But how is that possible? you might ask.

Well, you get crystal clear on where you are going, and you get super flexible on how you get there.

You get 100% clarity on what each other's strengths and passions are about the business and you delegate them accordingly.

And you openly discuss your parts of the business often.

Asking, *What is working? What isn't working? What I might do differently?*

It's no different from being in a corporate position, except here it's ok to sleep with your coworker!

At first, this was not how we approached our business. I was in the driver's seat, and had picked the opportunity (or at first, it picked me), and as things evolved, it led us to a couple of different opportunities; let's call it shiny object syndrome.

What we discovered was that this was the fastest way for one half of the partnership to lose passion for what we were doing.

At this time we were spending thousands of dollars on ads, training, and travel. Our business was starting to do the exact opposite of what we had hoped for: it was costing us money, consuming our time, and sucking the passion out of us

Stress was building, tensions were high, and the alignment was gone.

We knew we had to pivot again or it was not going to end the way we envisioned.

So this is where we get back to the passion and emotion part of building a business with your spouse.

We had to find the passion and reignite that emotion for both of us if we were going to keep going.

So we actually stepped away from it all to evaluate what we really wanted and how we were going to get there.

We looked closely at the opportunities available to us and we weighed the pros and cons.

We evaluated the people we would be surrounded with, and the training that they provided.

We made sure there was complete alignment for both of us, and made sure both of us could fit in, and share the driver's seat.

Through Carla's passion for helping others share their stories and my love of connecting with and serving other people, we found ourselves in a whole new world.

We found a way to focus all the training and mentorship we had and things were clicking.

We were back in alignment, but as always, the universe likes to throw us curve balls!

But this time we smashed it out of the park.

That curveball was TikTok—yes, I said it. TikTok.

We were super resistant to it, even to the point of taking it off our daughter's phone.

But a mentor we highly respect shared some info that grabbed our attention.

So we dove head first into action.

At first, it was slow, but all of a sudden things got wild.

10,000 followers
15,000 followers
80,000 followers

It was not slowing down and soon was over 100k

People messaging, *What are you doing? How do I get involved?*

Our business was cranking—it was unlike anything we'd ever experienced.

Then entrepreneurs and industry leaders started asking us to train their teams and their students. They wanted to know how we did it.

That sparked an idea... we had watched other friends build out coaching platforms and create massive success, so why couldn't we do that?

So we did just that.

We took everything we had learned; we clearly defined our roles in the business based on our passions and strengths and since then there has been no slowing down.

We have built a thriving community of marketers who want to leverage short-form video for their business. We have helped hundreds of people build their businesses through virtual training and speaking at live events and in under 10 months we created another 6-figure business.

The growth in our business has opened doors for our family that were otherwise closed and it is all because we stayed true to our ultimate goal and were connected to it on an emotional level.

We were open with each other, shared what we liked and did not like, and were willing to pivot when things were not going in the direction we wanted.

Business with your spouse should be fun, it should inspire you and give you more time with your family.

So if you take anything away from this we hope that you see it is possible to build a business with your partner.

You can also do it while you both have your own career; it is all about clear and open communication, finding and leveraging each other's strengths, and being sure you are energetically and emotionally connected to what you are doing so that when times get rough—and trust me they will—you will be able to navigate and make the pivots needed to keep you moving forwards, having fun, and most importantly in love.

Expert Tips:

How to Engage Family in Your Business

We run our own business to give us more money, more time, and more experiences with our families, but like anything worthwhile, it is going to take work. It is going to take sacrifice, time, and most likely it is going to present us with challenges.

Rome was not built in a day and your business won't be either. So as we start to go down the road of entrepreneurship and home business here are some tips on how to involve your family and create a thriving environment for them, you, and your business:

- We need to be clear with ourselves on what our goals are and how we are going to achieve them. Then we need to share that exact same information with our family. Let them know why you are doing what you are doing and what it is going to take for you to achieve that.

- Simple things like setting "working hours" where your family knows it is your time, and only to interrupt in the case of an emergency. Also let them know that sometimes, unexpected things can pop up, and flexibility during those times is appreciated.

- Let them know that you may have to hop on phone or zoom calls at random times.

- If you have an online business, let them know you are on your phone for business and you're not just scrolling on social media.

- Ask your family to help you achieve your goals by stepping in with chores to free you up to do income-producing activities.

- Ask your family what is important to them. What goals do they have that you can support and what are the non-negotiables? For example, mom comes to all soccer games on Wednesday nights but can miss practice.

- Most importantly, involve your family in the perks, benefits, and excitement your business brings. Can you win a trip? Share that and hang it on the fridge! If you hit a goal can you celebrate with a fun dinner or family outing?

- Simple, frequent, and open conversations can prevent conflict as you start and continue to build your business. This keeps your family in the tent—knowing what you are up to and why.

Setting these expectations and sharing these goals with your family will help you energetically, emotionally, and mentally, as the road of business building and entrepreneurship is often a windy and bumpy one, but when you have the support and encouragement from the ones you love most it will make all the difference in the world.

Angela Bell

Founder and CEO of The Inspired & Profitable Momprenuer

Angela Bell is the founder of The Mom Magic Anthology Series and the Mom Magic Movement! She is also the founder and CEO at The Inspired & Profitable Mompreneur Business, Podcast, Magazine, and TV Show.

Angela is on a mission to empower moms around the world to stand in their power, embrace their dreams, and create their own business!

Angela is a 6X International Best Seller, multi-passionate entrepreneur, business coach for moms, and mom of twins.

https://www.linkedin.com/in/angela-bell-776a529/
https://www.facebook.com/angela.bell.3597/
https://www.instagram.com/i.am.angelabell/
https://www.inspirednprofitablemompreneur.com/

LIFE IS ON THE OTHER SIDE OF FEAR!

By Angela Bell

My soul was dying.

I could feel it each and every day. Waking up with anxiety and dread. Rushing through the day from task to task, never stopping, barely able to remember what I had done moments before. I was tired—exhausted, really. My family wasn't getting the best version of me. Heck, they were getting the worst version. This couldn't be all there was to life. This couldn't be what I was born for, my purpose. Life couldn't be this meaningless…could it?

The worst part was, this wasn't the first time I'd felt this way. I was constantly switching from one profession to another, hoping each time it would be different. Don't get me wrong, I had a lot of external, superficial success symbols to show for it: I had a law degree, an MBA, a mortgage license; I had won awards, met with celebrities, consulted on government legislation. But the truth still remained—my soul was dying and it would take me with it.

My name is Angela Bell. I am happy to say that is not how it ended. But if I'm being honest, that period of my life lasted far longer than it should have. Which is why I felt called to write this chapter. So that you don't make the same mistake.

I am now living my purpose. I am a mompreneur success coach, mom advocate, 6X international best-selling author, anthology creator, and speaker. More importantly, I am happy, I am present with my children, and I am connected to my husband.

I always knew I was meant to do big things. Ever since I was a young child, I believed with everything in my heart that I was here to make a difference. I was here to help, to have an impact on the world, to leave it better than I found it.

I am a truth seeker. I believe in justice, fairness, kindness, and all the things we need more of in the world. For a while, I buried all of that deep down inside, because I was afraid.

Fear is funny that way; it's supposed to protect us from danger, but really it stops us from being our best selves.

I was afraid of failure, success, judgement, disapproval. You name it, deep down inside, I was afraid of it. It didn't make any sense, mind you. I was smart, pretty, successful. I succeeded at everything I tried. But like a lot of people, I suffered from imposter syndrome. I worried constantly that everyone else knew more than I did and that one day they were going to realize I didn't have a clue what I was doing.

All of my fears came true when my family business went bankrupt a year after my father died. There I was, the leader of a bankrupt company, a FAILURE.

Why am I telling you all of this? When I read back over these words, they don't sound all that inspiring. So, you may be asking yourself, what's the point?

The point is, it didn't matter. The point is, I made myself miserable for years, didn't go after my dreams, played small, and did what I thought people wanted me to do, because I was afraid of what people would think. And the truth is, they didn't care. The truth is, I am still here, standing strong and living my best life. One less-than-optimal outcome did not destroy me or the world, even if it was hard to go through. Everything I feared turned out to be not that scary, and I am freer for having experienced it. The great thing about the "worst" happening is that once it's over, you realize there is nothing left to fear. I am living proof that you will not die from failure; you will be reborn stronger, smarter, and more compassionate than before. So as a good friend of mine always says, "Fail often, fail fast, and fail cheap."

If you have a dream inside your heart that you aren't pursuing because of fear, I get it. I've been there. And it's time to let that shit go.

It took me some time, and a lot of inner work. I wish I could say that I had an epiphany and woke up one day different. I didn't, but I finally understand that I have to share my gifts. And so do you.

Your desires, dreams, and purpose were placed in your heart for a reason. It is not an accident or mistake that you want the things you want, or dream the dreams you dream. It was all placed with you for you to make it a reality. There is no one else in this whole entire world with your gifts. If you don't share them with the world your way, they will never be shared. Only you can do things your unique way. And the world needs that.

Looking back, that small business bankruptcy was probably exactly what I needed at the time. I didn't love running the business anymore. I was tired, but I was too afraid of disappointing people. So, the universe did for me what I could not do for myself. It got me out. The bankruptcy gave me the freedom to pursue other options. It forced me to look at my life and ask hard questions: How did it get this bad? What role did I play in all of this? And most importantly, what do I want?

Oftentimes we get so wrapped up in being who we think other people want us to be that we forget to ask ourselves who we want to be. It can be hard, with all the noise out there. So, ask yourself, "who do I want to be?" Don't rush the answer either. Another way to think about it is, if you were on an island alone, and you knew everyone and everything else was taken care of, what would you do?

When we strip away all the "shoulds" and "have tos", we get to the want to. And that is where you need to focus. What do you want to do? What matters to you? Or as my husband likes to say, "Everyone knows what they *don't* want Angela. What do you *want?*" Think on that for a while.

Now I empower moms. I help moms launch and grow their own online businesses so that they can live the lives they deserve. And I love it! I am making the world a better place by empowering the most influential group on the planet. I am helping mothers reclaim their worth, and in turn, breaking generational curses and empowering women as a whole. I help women share their stories and inspire other women. I spread hope, joy, and possibility. This gets me out of bed in the morning on fire. This makes my heart sing. This is exactly what I was meant to do.

You have a purpose, and it is beautiful. While the road isn't always easy, it is truly worth it.

Live a life that sets your soul on fire! It will light up the whole world!

Xo Angela

Expert Tips:

So how did I make this transformation? How did I go from a fear-based existence to living my purpose, following my true calling, and getting paid to help others do the same?

Firstly, I failed and survived. Going through small business bankruptcy, almost losing my house, living every business owner's biggest fear, showed me that there was nothing to be afraid of. Sure, it was hard. I ugly cried a lot through the process, but I'm stronger for it. And I didn't die. The world didn't end. Every terrible thing I thought would happen didn't. And I learned A LOT.

Next, look for the lessons. This can take time. When you are in the middle of feeling the sting of a less than optimal outcome, it can be hard to see the lessons. But once the dust has settled, look back and learn.

Be proud of the things you did do! No matter how bad it turns out, chances are you did some amazing things along the way. Celebrate those. Did you do something you've never done before? Awesome. Did you try new things? Amazing. Celebrate the good that did happen; I promise, it's not all bad.

Get comfortable being uncomfortable. It's just like any muscle. The more you do uncomfortable things, the easier they get. Make it a game. Challenge yourself to do something that scares you everyday. It will get easier, I promise!

Follow your Purpose!
#PurposeDrivenPaycheck
With Certified Success Coach Gina Redzanic

Purpose Driven Paycheck is an incredibly inspiring anthology created by Gina Redzanic featuring a total of 18 unique stories. Passing on our own expertise is an important part of "paying it forward" to those who aspire to follow their own passion and purpose. Each author has strengthened their credibility as an expert in their chosen field. In this book, the authors convey their confidence, depth of knowledge, and their 'hard-learned' success strategies to inspire their audience. Readers will find that the chapters within *Purpose Driven Paycheck* teach valuable opportunities for personal, professional, and creative development.

Looking for more business and income strategies?

Gina Redzanic offers business and success coaching,
affiliate opportunities, and can help build your brand with
published articles, ads, and social outlets.

For more information,
contact ginaredzanic@gmail.com
www.ginaredzanic.com

Featured in...

www.ingramcontent.com/pod-product-compliance
Lightning Source LLC
Chambersburg PA
CBHW071703210326
41597CB00017B/2303